Kille... ...

Sales

Techniques

How to sell Ice to

Eskimos and oil to Texans!
Guy Glas

ISBN: 9781674459974

DEDICATION

FOR LOUI

This BOOK Will Make You More Money,
Give You More Fun, Boost Your Career
and change your life for the better!

Speed learn to Sell what you want faster, easier and for more money

This Sales Encyclopaedia is written in plain English

Acknowledgments

Kristie Toombs for not only putting up with my frustrations but also proofreading and editing.

Wayne for telling me I should be a teacher.

Bill J for telling me to write a book.

Robbie A for being a Sales Gun and sharing his years of experience working for the fortune 500

Malcolm for trusting my expertise, and allowing me the opportunity to fill his Companies bank accounts with millions.

This book has been written with everyone in mind. If you think about it, every day you are selling!

If you're going out on a date, and you really like the person, you have to know how to sell..

If you want your dream job, you need to know how to sell.

If you're in business of any kind, you need to know how to sell.

To be successful, you first have to sell yourself, just like a job interview.

You have a duty to be successful, if what you're offering is good then you need to tell it to the world.
The methods used in this book are rooted in neuro linguistic programming to directly Target Prospects subconscious, completely by stealth and undetectable unless you've read the book :)

- Generate leads, using easy Neuro-linguistic programming techniques.

- Get appointments. - on the first call.

- Close sales. - at the first meeting

- Using Hypnosis tricks on your prospect, and nail the deal.

- Get a date or the Job of your dreams.

- ***The Secret Sales formula***.

- *Telemarketing.*

- **Sales letters** that won't end up in the trash.

- 25 of the most powerful ***magic words***

- Learn how to cold sell.

- Killer words to kill objections.

- Write ads.

- ***Mindpower.***

- ***Market yourself and your product*** effectively.

SO, WHO WANTS TO BE A MILLIONAIRE?

You do if you're not already.

Let's face reality: The same ways the wealthiest people have made their money. Earning and accumulating larger amounts of money, on an annual basis than hourly or salaried workers, and then reinvesting it (wisely), either in their own business or investments.

I'll leave out...

Full-time real estate investing, and the stock market (requires money upfront).

That leaves business ownership.

OH, and being great at sales.

That's right. One of the best ways for regular people to become millionaires is to excel in sales. Being in sales is like running your own business, without the investment and risk.

So you're a salesperson, or you're going to be one, this book will take you through Cold Canvassing to nailing the Deal or Job.

Inside this book

How to use mind power techniques to make your life what you want and get what you want.

Finding the most effective way to sell.

The Secret formula. I've noticed that many of the other books walk around but never spell out in black and white.

Telemarketing, getting to the right guy, the Decision Maker.

Sales letters that won't end up in the trash.

25 of the most powerful magic words the experts don't want you to know.

Cold calling, how to have a captive audience and not a door slam.

Cold calling an intercom.

The appointment. How to be treated like an old friend.

Objections and knock-backs, how to blow them away!

The close. Nice guys finish last. Close at least 70% more.

How to sell more and work less

<u>MANY PEOPLE GO TO COLLEGE OR UNIVERSITY FOR YEARS AND STILL DON'T EARN MORE THAN $1500.00 A WEEK!</u>

But you can, now for very little money, you can become a sales and marketing genius earning more than $50* per hour or more!

Inside this book, you will find the true sales formula, the one the others don't want you to know. Like a movie or a play, there is the RIGHT formula. When these techniques are engaged and fuelled by a powerful mind, These secrets work like magic. Once you learn the sales formula, they can be applied to about any situation, where you need to persuade others - to convince them to obey your commands.

You will learn how to have your prospects hang on your every word, and be ready to hand you the cash.

Sounds fantastic, doesn't it? Learn how to take control of every prospect. Have them listen to what you say and not let them shut you down.

And it works! (You read this far haven't you?)

Then learn how to close them

Sales is a psychological mind play if you're already a salesperson you will know exactly what I mean.

You know the publisher told me that we would get $100 per copy of this book. How much would you pay to spend a week or three with a sales and marketing professional? But you know what? I can see that you want to be more successful, so I'm going to help you. Please, please don't get all teary now, I still have to charge you something. No not $80.00 or $70.00 or even $60.00, we still have to pay the printers and the publisher and editor so....

Turn it over and have a look on the back.

Hey that's pretty good, isn't it! AND to make it even better, with no risk to you I will personally give you a...

100% Guarantee!

My promise to you is that this book will improve your sales, and cut to the chase (don't you hate those motivational books that ramble on and walk around the answers) or you will get a full refund within 7days of the purchase price when you take this book back to the place you brought it at, provided that is in a saleable condition. Stealing it doesn't count! (You should be able to read this book in 2 days).

So let's go toward your millions!

Why be limited by any figure?

A lot of people have trouble closing the deal, asking for the business, asking for the job. I've read lots of sales books and they're all pretty good, but sometimes I wonder if the publisher had asked them to make sure the book is 500 pages long. It doesn't have to be. It's obvious that you have to stay motivated, and confident, and friendly, and smile and welcome complaints, and objections, to handle them in a smooth calming manner.

All the tools you will ever need are in this book, the only thing you will need to bring to the table is bulldog determination. To stay mentally present, kill the negative self-talk, accept the fact that we live in an abundant universe.

CONTENTS

Chapter 1 - People are selfish pigs!

People are selfish pigs!

There is right now most likely a war going on somewhere, people are dying, bullets flying left, right, and centre, imagine the pain of copping a bullet from an assault rifle in the chest, imagine the difficulty in breathing your last few breaths. Imagine blood pulsing from the wound and the sharp stabbing pain that bites with every beat of your heart.

Now you're in the garage repairing a wooden crate to put some junk in and you hit your thumb with the hammer and you say a few choice words. What about the war? Who gives a damn about the war?

Selective worry. It is human nature to have a worry or three, now if your grandmother was ill, you would be worried about her. But the moment you hit your thumb you only have that on your mind. Your spouse may have a splitting headache that hurts more than your thumb, but hey, you can't feel it!

So what does this mean?

Ever met someone who walked up to you at a party or gathering and said "Hi I'm Joe, I'm in the furniture business here is my card. We do the furniture restorations for the government parliament you know!"

You would have an instant dislike for this type of guy. Because you are interested in you, and he is interested in him. But what about when someone introduces himself like....

"Hi I'm John, you are?"

"Mike" you respond

"So what do you do Mike?"

"I'm in sales."

"What kind of product is it that you sell?"

"Oh I sell fireplaces"

"Wow, now that's something different, I never really thought about having to be sold a fireplace I just assumed you go and buy one at a fireplace shop. Do you sell the wood-burning ones or is everything gas these days?"

" Well no John fireplaces come in different styles, and..."

So here you can see you are getting along just fine with John and you would probably sell him a fireplace. You like John because he is a warm and friendly guy. Let's go back to the conversation for a moment.

" So Mike (that's you), you like to go fishing on the weekend, have you ever fished at twilight bay?"

So now John is getting more and more information from you.

" John, you haven't told me what you do?"

" Sorry Mike, I am an electrician."

"Do you work for yourself?"

"Well yes I do Mike"

" What would you charge me to put a light bulb fitting in my garage John?"

"Well, I would have to see what's involved, but I'll do you a good deal."

"When could you come over?"

Now what happened here John (your new buddy) just sold you.

Why? Because he built a relationship with you, he befriended you, he gained your trust and sold you.

This is called rapport building.

Rule no 1

YOU WON'T SELL ANYTHING TO ANYONE IF YOU DON'T MAKE FRIENDS FIRST!

This rule sticks, whether on the phone, cold call or a warm sale, and this goes through the whole process.

So you have to sell yourself first!

I really believe that if you're selling a service, it's best not to have salesperson or salesman or business development manager on a business card. Part of my pitch when selling services is on the first instance of voice contact I mention that "this is not a sales pitch, this is to see if we are a good fit, you are going to be interviewing the services, features & benefits of creating a relationship with us, and I will be doing the same with you, I wanted to take this time so we can sit as acquaintances and leave as friends, just to have a discussion of how we can help".

This helps to lower their natural negative resistance to having something pushed on them.
you really want to be able to keep your relationship that way.

People will judge you in the first 30 seconds of meeting you. (Look your best and be smiling).

Everyone needs to sell at some point.

If you can't sell you can't get a good job.

If you can't sell you can't hire staff that will stick by you.

If you can't sell you can't market your product.

Now that we know people are basically selfish, how do we use this to our advantage? Easy Cater to their ego!

You want to force a good vibe, we all remember people who are just constantly miserable and this is an extreme example.
However, people tend to stay away from the sad sacks.
It has happened to me in personal life when talking to my partner about throwing a Halloween party.
We sat there with our list of friends on the computer thinking who to invite, if you've ever done this, you'll know what I'm talking about.

The character traits of the person, you see on your list come up for discussion.

"Sue, Jane, Mike, they are all really fun let's make sure we invite them first, oh what about Steve, he tends to get a bit argumentative after a few drinks. let's see how we go for numbers and put him at the bottom of the list. What about Bianca, although it would be good for her she is just miserable, and antisocial she might bring down the Vibe when engaging some of our other friends talking about her problems."

So what is the first thing you would do before you say " Hi my name is _____ from Company xyz have you seen this great vacuum cleaner.. here's my business card, its only $599.00

Now, this is the right way, you will have to win them over more if you cold call (there is a better way for phone calls).

Cold call House

Hi I'm _____ From Company XYZ, how are you today? WOW, that's a nice garden/ car/ doorbell chime/ roof job/ lawn etc must have taken you ages to look after that, I can see you are very smart and skilled, did you do the lawn/ garden yourself? Wow etc, etc

Appointment

Hi I'm _____ From Company XYZ, I am here to see Mr Ms _____.

Hi Mr Ms _____, how are you today pardon me for asking but that's a nice suit / dress your wearing where did you get that? (*Safest used on same-sex*) It's nice to finally meet you! How long have you been working here? What is your actual role in the company? Oh you're a _____ that must be a very important position … etc

Or at a house.

Wow, that's a nice garden/ car/ doorbell chime/ roof job/ lawn etc.. Must take you ages to look after that, I can see you are very smart and skilled did you do the lawn/ garden yourself? Wow etc, etc

Or if you went there last week and meet the person before

Hi, Mr Ms_____ How are you? _____From Company XYZ, I saw you last week about _____, have you lost weight, you must be working out? Great day / Evening isn't it?

This is probably extreme but you get the idea, if said sincerely, flattery will 90% of the time get you everywhere, you can even complement someone if you are in retail, or...

Tele-marketing. Tell them they have a great phone voice! You should do audio-books for a job. Or they sound like a DJ (for a man). You have to learn to think on your feet and try not to be too cheesy.

WARNING: don't overdo it. You can talk about current events, like what did you think about the football score last night or the yacht race or anything, that you can talk about for two-four minutes before you sell them anything!

There was a time when I was selling a vending machine service. Instead of walking into the office, and handing a business card over announcing would you like a vending machine when it's very likely they already have one.

The first thing I would say would be, " I want you to imagine for a moment, and really visualise yourself on a holiday in Thailand. You're kicking back on the beach listening to the waves crash having a few of your favourite beverages. you start to feel hungry, so you head over to that little restaurant and you have the most amazing Thai curry chicken it was really cheap.
Now I can bring that to you. Imagine getting a healthy Chinese, Indian, Japanese, healthy nutritionally balanced meal, and a drink, for under $9? Our company does that, in a very specialised vending machine right next to your coke and Mars Bars.
Now I would like to introduce myself and ask for the managers business card so that I can send over a menu via email.
Sometimes I would walk in with a cheap small bag of lollies.
 I often imagine by the look on the receptionist's face when you walk in with a folder on your arm, are they mentally saying, "who the fuck is this, not another sales rep."
Sometimes I would take a few and just hand them out in the office, it would always bring a smile to their face and break down the initial negative barrier.
Sometimes I would continue on about the technology, straight away I am raising interest.

When it came time to call the manager after sending a few emails with some information, I would call up and say "Hey John, it looks like I owe you that free lunch."

John is thinking "who the fuck is this?"
 I would further explain that "not only do I have... Thai lunch for him but a huge bag of chocolates and chips."

"A few days ago I sent you some emails John, about a very special service, it's a free thing I'm not selling anything but your staff are very keen on this idea so I'd love to come over tomorrow about 10 am and drop off this huge sack of food and have a quick chat."
I'm not asking the guy I'm telling him!

Sometimes you would be hit with a place that did not even have a receptionist, they might just have an intercom.

Push the button on the intercom and say, "I just want to leave you a menu".

Or "Package for you."

You have to break down your sales into steps, if there is no one there your first goal is to just get someone to open the door. When they open the door, freely walk inside don't give them the opportunity to take control. Hand them a bag of lollies or a small gift, don't just hand over one of your promo pens, if it's wrapped in a box with a bow on it it's more of a surprise.

I probably wouldn't do this if it was a house.
If it has a camera, try to hide from it, or just show your face and not the logo on your shirt.

I don't advocate trespassing, some places are like Fort Knox, I would throw on the high visibility vest, tuck the folder under the arm and wait for the electronic gate to open when another car was coming in. It's surprising how far you can get when you look like you're supposed to be there, I wouldn't even ask the staff where the manager was, hand over a bag of lollies, or even be pointed in the direction of where the Vending machines were.

At the meeting

So you've gone through the process of finding qualified leads. You've called them and made an appointment. You have isolated the decision-maker. If it was a cold call you can plant the seeds at the time when you're speaking to another staff member or even the receptionist.

"Simply ask who is the person in charge of making the decisions about this product?"

If you can convince the receptionist that your item is a good idea, on occasion they will simply produce the boss's business card. A lot of times, you'll be met with, " I will pass these details on."

A customer will rarely ring you, I've had executive assistants, that will take information from me, and come across as genuinely excited about a product. When I say, "Can I email you some further information?"
and they have even said, "I don't have a business card but you can write this down?"
I have occasionally found myself, falling into the trap of saying, "Take my card, and email me now." Don't leave without an email or phone number, if you have left without an email or phone number you might have to find someone else in the building. Either that, or come back in a week or two, but not leaving without contact details will set you back. If the prospect is in front of the computer when you are canvassing you might be able to get them to email you on the spot but perhaps ask for them to write it on a post-it note just in case there is a problem with the email.

The next step is to sit down and have a meeting.

If you go in to have the meeting and you are met with a lower level of staff simply ask them if the decision-maker could join us, as although things are quite simple, many questions will arise best addressed on the spot.

One very interesting psychological trick that I have learned from a friend who was the national sales manager for a Fortune 500 company until he decided to go out on his own, is that you can almost talk about anything when you were walking with someone to a meeting room or across the factory floor, and 99% of the time they will answer you honestly. However, when you sit down it's about to become ' all business.'

If they bring you into the meeting room do not sit straight away, wait for them to sit and then choose the spot at a 90-degree angle. If it is a round table, DO NOT sit across from them.
People do this subconsciously by creating a magical barrier between you and them, so they can 'Dodge your missiles.'

Depending on the character type, the best way to move forward here is to say something funny and have a bit of a general chit-chat for a couple of minutes before hooking into your presentation.

Most of the time, with most people, you want to tell a story some features and benefits about your product from two separate angles. From years of experience, men like to know the technical details how fast? the how? and fuel economy. Women want to know what it's practical use is, what colour it comes in, the aesthetics and how it will fit into the workplace and even what is it's environment impact.
You want to anchor things in your story.
".. for instance, the other day when I was with our Fortune 500 client so-and-so, this particular thing happened, and we were able to take care of that by providing this solution."

Work necessary information into the story, your goal is to explain to them how your product is the best latest and greatest but also you have some pretty big hitters as clients. This is a much better method than simply saying "Oh we have 10 of the biggest companies in the world as clients and we have this really cool thing that's really expensive."

You don't want to come across as a braggart, you want to come across as someone who has some really interesting information through a story.

When you're nearing the end of your presentation don't forget to start the yes ladder, aka tie-downs and trial closes. (More depth on these techniques later).

What if your job is to **sell to** someone who is inquiring about your product?

Let's look at this scenario

Telephone rings

" Hello Joes tyre repairs, Mike speaking how may I help you?"

"How much is a Tyre for a Ford van"

"$80.00"

"Thank you bye"

Now that customer will just keep ringing up tyre shops until they either work out that all tyres are in the $60-$90 range and buy the cheapest, or they find a friend who will care and comfort them and love and cuddle them and tell them that it's all going to be OK.

Now let's look at the best way

Telephone rings

" Hello Joes tyre repairs, Mike speaking how may I help you? "

"How much is a Tyre for a Ford van"

" How did it happen? "

"I was driving down the expressway and a nail went through it"

" That's terrible, did you control the car OK? "

"It swerved a bit, but not too much loss of control"

" Is everyone OK? "

"The wife was a little shaken"

" You know the best way is to pull over and try not to brake hard just coast to a stop. "

"That's exactly what I did."

" It's a good thing you're a man in control, we get to hear some real nasty stories here! Now how bad is the tyre? "

"Well it's just flat."

"We would probably be able to repair that, could you show it to me?"

" Well yes, when could I come in. "

" I could see you in about 2 hours, or is tomorrow better? "

"No I'll come over soon."

" Great I'll see you soon then. "

Now just by making friends you got him in the shop!

Getting in the door and getting them in your door is 55% of the battle won!

People don't understand the nature of their problem, your job in sales is to identify a problem, and find a solution.

The customer's problem is that they need the vehicle to get to work, what has happened here is an inconvenience. You need to care about that problem.

I was in business with a radiator repair & manufacturing Factory.

People would ring up and say how much is a radiator for a ' insert vehicle model here'.

The minute I told them the price they would say thank you and hang up.
So instead, I would inquire as to what the problem was, mentioning I could probably fix it for $30. A lot of times they would show up at the workshop, the Radiator would be beyond repair. But, walking them through what the problem is and offering a solution, and also comparing that to a cheap fix would have them spending premium dollars with me.

What kind of sale

Definitions of sales

1. The nastiest of all is the **cold call (cold canvassing).**

2. The **Telemarketing**. Where you ring them and try to flog them something, that up to now, they didn't need!

3. The **appointment** or **warm call.**

4. The **warm sale.**

5. The **hot prospect**!

- The nastiest of all is the **cold call.** This is when you knock on someone's door or walked into his or her office, Workshop/ Factory they will instantly dislike you because you disturbed them.

- The **Telemarketer.** Don't worry everyone hates a phone salesperson, just as much but if you're good you can keep them on the phone.

- The **appointment** or **warm call.** This is where you (or someone else) has/have made an arrangement for you to see them because they are mildly interested in what you or your company does.

- The **warm sale.** Too easy! They are keen to have what your selling or one of your other customer told them about what you do.

- The **hot prospect**! They just want it!

Definitions of results
1. No good - **NG**
2. Knock-back - **KB**
3. Call back -**CB**
4. Closed Sales -**CS**
5. Fail -**F**

- A **No good is** when you go through your whole presentation and they just won't sign or they say it sounds great but no.

- A **Knock-back** is when they shut you down straight away and hang up and shut the door.

- A **Call back** is when they just can't make up their mind now because "they have a lot on their plate"

- A **Closed Sales** your ultimate goal

- A **Fail** they don't qualify for your product! They either have one or just won't use it (like trying to sell a skateboard to an 80-year-old lady with a walking frame, But I'm sure she has grand kids keep trying).

Later on, I'll equip you with the tools you need and show you how to blow away 90% of the knock backs, no goods and call-backs and turn them into **Closed sales.**

Before I show you the secret formula for sales, we first have to look at goals.

Chapter 2 - How do you set a goal and how do you stick to it?

Goal setting is very, very, very, very important. The most successful businessmen will tell you that. Set a target and stick to it, schedule your time and stick to it (just don't over commit).

For example

If you know that selling vacuum cleaners, door to door will give you $70 commission per unit before tax and you want to earn $1400.00 before tax every week then you know that you must sell 20 units per week, or 4 a day. Which is roughly one every 2hours, discount travelling time and NGs, KBs, and CB's, that leaves you a comfortable hour and a half for your presentation and close, which could be trimmed to an hour? Inside that hour try to structure your opener, presentation, trial closes, and touch down into segments. Structuring your hour will take practice because some customers will need more time with different parts, the best idea is to practice scenarios with another sales team member, your team manager (if you have one), a friend or spouse.

Aim high with your goals, there is an old saying that says, "If you aim for the moon you might hit a rock, but aim for the stars and you just might hit the moon!"

Set goals for the whole week and schedule your time. These days a lot of computer office software comes bundled with a Scheduler (Microsoft Outlook' has one), I use it religiously.

If you work for a bigger company you might look at customer relationship management software or CRM.

My time consists of writing for 2-3 hours a day, an hour work out most days, I do Marketing consultation weekday mornings, evening courses and make enough time to spend with my girl. Then occasionally I like to paint, watch TV and go to the movies. So as you can see if my time is not organised correctly I would miss my workouts and writing and all kinds of stuff.

Purchase of a Decent Smartphone, and using a calendar app has the facility to remind you of your long term goals, like having saved enough money for a new car or holiday or better still some long term investments like shares or property.

Once your subconscious is pumped with your conscious goals, your mind will be on autopilot, ready to focus on the issues at hand.

Remember the first time you tried to drive a car or ride a bike? How when the car felt like it was huge, and it took you awhile to get used to the dimensions before you were able to steer correctly, and if it was a stick shift, what was that like! Now you jump in your car, turn the key and wind up at your destination, sometimes not even knowing how you got there. This is how your mind works, do you remember how you learnt to speak. You probably don't. What about learning another language? Most of us would find that a very involved process. If you reinforce your goals every morning and night, your goals become second nature. **Later there is a whole chapter on the power of the mind and how to harness it.**

INVEST IN YOURSELF

How much money do you blow on inappropriate toys? How much did you spend last year on eating out, or drinking with your friends, or movies? Exactly how much will any of that contribute towards you being a millionaire? And how much did you invest in your own sales self-improvement last year? I constantly see sales reps beating their heads against the wall experiencing needless rejection. It's not that difficult and a lot more fun to say and do things that get success on the phone (or anywhere else).

Your long term goals must be financial

Set achievable goals for a fixed amount of money by a certain date. Then work backwards so that every day is a step closer to your goal. Plan your life, and know you are on target. Don't over commit. Sure, everyone WISHES they had more money; few people have a specific goal with detailed plans for doing so. Personally, be sure to pay yourself first, regardless of how much it hurts. Set aside a percentage of everything you earn and sock it away. No excuses, no cheating. Like you say in the next 5 years I'll have $40,000 that's 8k a year $666 a month by saving $155.00 a week. If you are making good money in your sales job like over $1200 per week this should be possible. Just remember to pay your savings account before you pay for food, power, everything. Just remember to budget. If you earn less, then save less. Earn more, save more.

The more you sell, the more you earn, the more you invest, the more quickly it snowballs.

DON'T ASSUME YOU CAN'T DO ANYTHING

If you must doubt anything, doubt your limitations. Instead of saying, "I'm not sure I could accumulate a million dollars," instead, ask yourself this question, "What will I need to do to accumulate a million dollars in cash, assets net worth by (pick a date)?" be logical. If you earn $1200 per week and it cost you $500 a week to live you should be able to save $600 a week for your million ($100 put away for other stuff) it's going to take 2000 weeks to reach $1,000,000 or 38 and ½ years. If you don't want to wait that long you would start with say $250,000 and buy some real estate this could be done with a few years of saving. You would also invest in stocks etc.

My Barber was worth $3,000,000.00 in 1989, he lost most of it in a divorce. By 1999 he was worth 3.3m.

How? Real estate, shares, and term deposits. Not though cutting hair, although he has to cut hair to have an income and accrue the money. He is not a barber, he is a property developer.

Do you think Mc Donald's are in the business of making hamburgers? Mc Donald's set up a restaurant on a big slice of property, then lease it to a manager. The manager (investor) coughs up $1,000,000 upfront, and lease the premises of Mc Donald's. Mc Donald's pays the bank and sells off the rest of the land to whoever will buy it. Service stations, shops, or even KFC!

Then start answering the question. Brainstorm. Write down your answers. You might be surprised how realistic and tangible answers become when you take away the false limitations of your own thinking. It was a common problem in selling that when I came across a big customer I would get nervous, and sometimes blow the sale.

For example, in the 90's I was selling a new type of phone door to door. This phone was a mobile and home phone in one package when at home the calls were at a local rate, and when out of the house and yard in turned into a mobile phone. A great idea! One great bonus is that you could use the home number to call the customer anywhere. The other is that they had a great new cordless phone that became a second phone when the first line was tied up with fax or Internet. Anyway, for every handset, I sold I got $40. In the beginning, I would just sell each customer that qualified, one phone as a second line, the average night was two customers or $80. Most jobs at the time Paid $100 per day. The phone cost $29 for one, cheap enough, but if the customer wanted more it was $9 for every unit after that (limited to 4). So instead of saying "This is the phone, it does this and this and that".

Now If you are currently in sales you will know when a customer is interested, (if you haven't got it yet, it will come). After explaining the features and benefits of the phone, I would say, "How many people use the phone that live or stay here?" and they would say just me, or my wife and I, or 3 or 4. Then I would reply, "We are doing a package deal on these great phones and since it's just you at home you get 2 for $38.00! One for use as a second phone Great if someone stays over, and one to take out with you, Fantastic Hey? Sign here… we are delivering on Monday and Tuesday, which day will suit you? Great, thank you and enjoy your new phones."

The ideal market for this was a family all under the age of 50 with teenagers that tie up the phone, with a big house and expensive cars in the driveway. I would knock on the doors and get a single mum and she would buy a phone or I would get a young couple who would be in and out of the house at different times and sell them one each. But out of the times when people were not home, older people, and single people that were in a mobile phone contract, finding that big house was like an oasis that could turn a $40 night into 5-6 phones or $160 for a night or 4 hours work.

SELL MORE TO EXISTING ACCOUNTS

How many of your customers buy the exact same things you sell, from someone else? Why couldn't you get a bigger piece of the pie? Again, our biggest limitation is normally our own small thinking and effort.

GO AFTER BIGGER SALES

Someone is selling to the bigger accounts. Why shouldn't it be you?

ASK for more, ALL OF THE TIME

It takes the same number of words to ask for a $1000 sale as it does a $500 deal from the same customer. As long as they were up to it, why not ask larger? Ok, say they go for just $750 instead of $1000. That's now $250 better than you would have been with the $500 deal. Put your extra profits away and buy some property.

The ultimate goal is to buy one house pay it off, or most of it, then loan against it, get house number 2 rent it out. Which means your tenants pay off your second house. Then do it again, why not buy a factory and lease it. If you buy enough of the right property you won't have to work any more! Along the way to buy and sell some shares.

Chapter 3 - The formula

1. **Make friends and create a relationship.**

2. **Disturb.**

3. **Relax them.**

4. **Show them what you have, paint a mental picture.**

5. **Features & benefits. Trial close.**

6. **Disturb then relax.**

7. **Create a high perceived value.**

8. **Relax them with a discount (or special deal). Trial close.**

9. **Throw in a bonus to close the deal.**

Explanations

The other day a few years ago, I went to the shopping mall to pick up a couple of things, and there was this guy standing on a platform about a foot off the ground, with a bench in front of him and one of those headset microphones on his head, (like Anthony Robbins). **He had a nice hair cut and quite fit-looking**, almost the male model type. The 'stage' he had set was complete with floodlights, and on the table was an assortment of cheese veggies and fruit. Yep, you guessed it a *salesman* flogging the latest kitchen wiz-bang gadget! I said to myself, I'll have to hang around for this...

The salesman notices I was waiting, and he was waiting until someone's mind was curious to wait and watch. Then he says "Hi everybody I'm Ken how is everyone today? What I'm about to show you will save you a lot of time and pain."

The salesman 'Ken' picks up your typical oblong, but slightly tapered cheese grater. Ken demonstrates the thumbnail rasp side, the pin punch side, the mini rasp and the little square blade. A crowd gathers around

"This side makes long shaving style strings of cheese and carrot, and sometimes knuckle skin. The pin punch side makes sawdust gratings and as you can see is also very difficult to push."

" Now this is the new Ezi-grate. Ezi-grate does the work for you, just put the block of cheese inside, pop the lid on and take it straight to the table, twist the top and the cheese comes out at the size you want just like a pepper grinder! Now you can have a fresh grate anytime, no more yucky powdered cheese. Marvellous, Huh? Like Parmesan and mozzarella? No problem! The Ezi-grate has 2 compartments, now you can mix cheese easy! If you like cheese and carrot blended shavings presto! Not only Carrot and cheese, but you can also now make hash browns the easy way to keep the skin on your knuckles. Now because it has a lid, Now there is no more waste, now that's a good idea, isn't it? Just pop it in the fridge for fast fresh pasta topping!"

"I can see you are all impressed, but this great new time-saving device, and you want to know how much it cost right? Well if you watch a lot of Television you would know that this splendid little skin saver sells at $30.00 and will save you that much in first aid strips. Now you think I'm going to give you a discount, you would pay $20 wouldn't you? But today, I'm going to let you have it for only $10!! That's right ten bucks. But better than that if you take it now I'll give you two!!!!"

Well, I have to tell you I couldn't pay the guy quick enough! And I still have the cheese grater. I've only used it twice but what a great invention! I still buy the powdered Parmesan cheese because it keeps longer.

NOW we will see how the formula was applied

The salesman looks good he has an instant likability. Then he says "Hi everybody I'm Ken how is everyone today? What I'm about to show you will save you a lot of time and pain."-

1.*Makes friends and creates a relationship.*

The salesman 'Ken' picks up your typical oblong, but slightly tapered cheese grater. Ken demonstrates the thumbnail rasp side, the pin punch side, the mini rasp and the little square blade. A crowd gathers around

"This side makes long shaving style strings of cheese and carrot, and sometimes knuckle skin. The pin punch side makes sawdust gratings and as you can see is also very difficult to push."- *2. He disturbs, creates a 'what's going on situation'.*

" Now this is the new Ezi-grate. Ezi-grate does the work for you, just put the block of cheese inside, pop the lid on and take it straight to the table, twist the top and the cheese comes out at the size you want just like a pepper grinder! *3. Relief*

4. Shows you what the product is. - Now you can have a fresh grate anytime, no more yucky powdered cheese. Marvellous, Huh? Like Parmesan and mozzarella? No problem! The Ezi-grate has 2 compartments, *5. feature*

"Now you can mix cheese easy! If you like cheese and carrot blended shavings presto! Not only Carrot and cheese, but you can also now make hash browns the easy way to keep the skin on your knuckles". _**5. benefit**_

Now because it has a lid, Now there is no more waste, *now that's a good idea, isn't it? –**Trial close**

Just pop it in the fridge for fast fresh pasta topping!"

"I can see you are all impressed by this great new time-saving device, and you want to know how much it cost right? –**_Trial close_**

Well if you watch a lot of Television you would know that this splendid little skin saver sells at $30.00 **_disturb and relax 7. High perceived value_**

and will save you that much in first aid strips. Now you think I'm going to give you a discount, you would pay $20 wouldn't you? But today, I'm going to let you have it for only $10 that's right ten bucks. _**8.Relax them with a discount**_

But better than that if you take it now I'll give you two!!!!"- _**9. throw something in getting a commitment and put them over the moon!**_

There is a little more to the psychology of sales than this, however, that's the formula

There can be objections raised-

Later I will explain trial closes and how to handle objections but for now, let's look at another scenario, and you can work out what is happening and when, I'll help you by putting in an asterisk* when part of the formula is in use as a clue, ready?

You're watching late-night TV and the advertisement for the new Non-stick fry pan comes on. 'The fat-free supa cooker'. The first line is what's called a door opener.

Voice over "Are you sick and tired of burning an omelette?
Sick of cleaning up a greasy mess ?*"

Host " Hi I'm Steve, and this is the new fat-free Supa cooker* Notice first of all it has a triple coated polymer Teflon layers* guaranteed for 5 years* which need absolutely no oil* even burnt milk just wipes off! Fantastic!" *

Switches to a video of burnt milk wiping off.

"The new fat-free Supa cooker has a thicker aluminium base that holds more heat and because it holds more heat you can use the new fat-free Supa cooker as an oven. You can see these holes around the rim in this countersunk edge when you place the high top lid on, you can roast a chicken inside.* This feature will save you money on your power bill* the holes work like a convection oven. Isn't that brilliant?" *

Video shows red arrows rotating around a cutaway of a Supa cooker.

"You can even roast on an oven rack accessory, that you can place the potatoes on, this converts to a steamer."

The steaming accessory fits in the fat-free Supa cooker.* Now you will know that most double steamers take over 45 minutes to steam cook, well with the fat-free Supa cooker just place the water in the bottom and your veggies on the top and the lid on and you can have healthy steamed veggies in 7 mins *"

" So you want to make a fast cheese and veggie omelette? Put your fat-free Supa cooker on the stove and warm it up. Mix your eggs and milk with a whisk, like you normally would, and pour the mix into the fat-free Supa cooker. Now here is the trick, flip over the steamer accessory, you will notice the steamer now comes a good inch higher than the pan. See that the steamer has a grater and a blade and a rasp on it, now as the omelette is cooking grab your cheese block and grate the cheese onto you omelette surface. Now grate your onion and garlic, use the slicer for thin carrots, chives, ham etc. lift the lid off and fold the omelette over so that the cheese and veggies cook and presto a gourmet omelette that would make a professional chef cry." *

Voice over " Now how much would you expect to pay for a fat-free Supa cooker? But wait! We will give you the steamer dish and the roast rack as well. So how much would you expect to pay for fat-free Supa cooker? For just $20 for the next four weeks, you can have healthier meals starting in three days. That's right for just $80 we will deliver to your door in three working days, the fat-free Supa cooker, the steamer/grater accessory, and the roast rack!"*

"CALL NOW, and receive a high top spacer ring for free. That's right! We will give you this spacer ring absolutely free, with the spacer ring you can roast a full-size turkey. But wait there's more! We will actually give you two! That's right we are going to give you 2 fat-free Supa cookers for just $80 and the steamer and the roast rack! And if you are one of the first 50 callers we will give you, absolutely free, the fat-free Supa cooker cookbook, over 80 secret recipes that will turn you into a master chef in minutes. CALL NOW!"

I enjoy watching those sales pitches that are purely an Internet video.

The same pattern can be found.

How to make thousands of dollars by selling kids books on Amazon.

Get a passive income.

It's easy.

The video goes to show how a simple story with only 200 words and some great imagery can be created on a weekend by finding a graphic designer to do the images for under $100 and how you put the whole thing together and publish it on Amazon.

Before the price is mentioned for the course, the obstacles are put forth, on how it's difficult to create the right file format, how it's difficult to get reviews.

The video goes on to show how the digital product is included software and sources to solve these problems.

The presenter then explains how his consulting fees for each part over $1,000 per Solution.

All of this adds up to some astronomical figure (disturbing and applying pressure, do you think that this wonderful, get rich easy program is now unattainable).

Then the presenter builds rapport by explaining that he knows you can't really afford that kind of money so he's going to do a special deal but only if you react quickly.

"I know you're struggling and I want to really help you out, so what I am going to do is take this whole package that has each section that I normally sell for $1,000 each, and that you would normally pay $7,000 if you were to engage me for all of these on a part by part basis. I'm going to do the whole thing for $499." (Presenter applies pain and then relief and validating the content of the product).

"Now you would have to agree that anyone can afford that?" (trial close).

"To make it even better, I'm going to throw in absolutely free how to convert your book into an audiobook, and in addition I'm going to allow you special access to a group of authors that can help in reviewing your freshly published book, I normally charge $700 for enrolling into my secret group and $200 for the software that converts text into any format, I'm going to throw all this in for free"

(presenter adds value).

Then the presenter goes on to add a few more things into the mix for free. "it's a fantastic deal isn't it?"

"I can't really afford to do this for too long so, the offer will only be available for the next 3 days, of course, you can get the course at a later time but it will be without the bonuses"

Make friends. If you can't do this then don't be a salesperson, this comes right down to how you look and sound. There is a whole book on this subject, called "How To Win Friends and Influence People. By Dale Carnegie." Every salesperson should read this book. Look at yourself in the mirror, would you buy something from you? Moreover, would a little old lady buy something from you? What about a fit person? Like it or not, first impressions are visual.

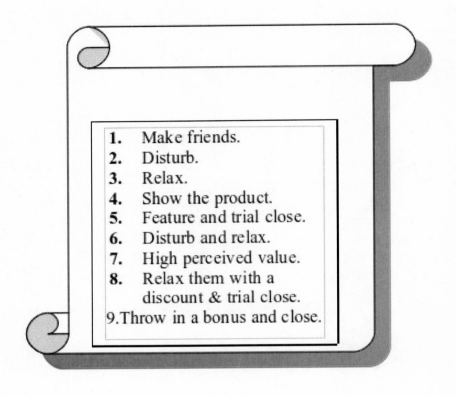

1. Make friends.
2. Disturb.
3. Relax.
4. Show the product.
5. Feature and trial close.
6. Disturb and relax.
7. High perceived value.
8. Relax them with a discount & trial close.
9. Throw in a bonus and close.

Any company that doesn't let its staff sell this way is not selling as much as they could!

Every professional TV shopping company, Mail order Company in the world that sells to a mass-market uses these techniques, and now that you know them you will see it for yourself.

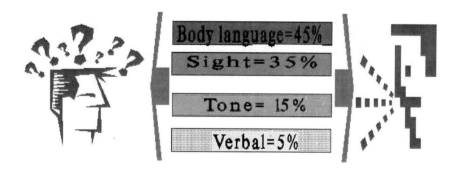

The order in which we access others is...
1. Body language

- Stance

- Gesture

- Facial expression

- Eye contact

- Personal space

2. Sight

- Colour

- Gender

- Age

- Dress

3. Tone

- Rate of speech

- Volume

- Pitch

- Articulation

4. Verbal

- What you're actually saying

Body language and sight can happen in different orders, as to if the person is introduced to you, or if you are similar to the person you are meeting. For example, if you are a working-class person and you meet a salesman in a suit you may feel like this person is in a different league, and it was the first thing you look at. Whereas if the person was the same height and age and in similar clothing to what you wear, you would look at their stance, gender, colour etc.

Thine will be judged

Preconception

Your friend tells you about a new person they have met, this person's name is Sue. Immediately, every Sue you know starting with the one you know most will pop into your head. Now if your friend talks about Sue a whole lot, when you finally meet Sue, she is nothing like your mental image! Now you are set back, you may even dislike Sue because she did not live up to your mental image.

If you are cold calling or meeting someone for the first time, they will try to find some common ground, starting with how you look and move.

Body language

Stance- Try to look relaxed, don't fold your arms, this is a negative gesture. Instead, stand with your palms up. This denotes that you're an honest person.

Gesture – Use your hands to speak remember that people are looking at you at not really listening. Point to your product, show them your display book / Flyer / Presentation

Facial expression- First of all smile. And when you say "That's a good feature, isn't it?" Nod your head in agreement, and create a subconscious agreement from your customer. Even the best liars will have a facial tick of some kind or even just pupil dilation. People don't always consciously pick up a lie, but they would have a gut feeling not to trust you. The best thing is don't lie in your presentation, it usually backfires. Remember, bad news travels faster than good news.

Eye contact- Look em in the eye, a lookup to the right means they are referring to a previous event. For example, when you ask someone when was the last time they had their car tuned they look to their right (some people may look from the opposite, this may be because they are left-handed or right brain creative types). If you ask them to do maths or spell they usually look up, like referring to the mind. Don't stare out your customer, and don't avoid eye contact either. Stare at a dog or ape in the eye and the animal is going to want to rip your head off. This is a sign of aggression in the animal kingdom. Find a steady normal eye contact, just like talking to a friend.

Personal space- In urban areas, people are used to close contact, due to the high density. In the country, personal space is a critical matter. Imagine your sitting at a bus stop, by yourself and someone you don't know sat right next to you so that you were less than a centimetres away. You would probably feel quite disturbed. If your working in non-city areas, remember to space yourself a bit more than you normally would in the city.

Sight

Colour- This you can't change, and why should you. But remember that as a salesperson, if you are a different colour than the majority, in a country or area of that country. You may find some people who feel a bit uneasy with you. This may require a bit of extra work from you, to gain the customer's confidence.

Gender- For most things women actually sell better than men, this may be because they might appear less of a threat than a male, however people selling in an area that is usually dominated by the other sex usually fail. For example, if you were getting some mechanical work done on your car, most people would trust a man before a woman. Just as in an area like childcare, you would more likely trust a woman's knowledge. Just like lingerie, and hair and beauty industries. In a modern world everyone is expected to treat other people fairly regardless of race or colour or religion, the simple fact is, many people will act like they are on board with this concept but secretly they might not be, as a salesperson you need to be appealing to everyone, well at least your prospects demographic. An extreme example of this would be selling tickets to a gay nightclub, if you are not gay then you would at least have to act like it.

Age- I reckon the younger you look better, However, an eighteen-year-old guy won't make a good real-estate salesman, because clients may view him as inexperienced. Just as a 60-year-old fellow selling Gaming or Skateboards. (There are of course exceptions, obviously if the skateboard guy, is a known professional celebrity, he's going to have exceptional street cred).

Dress- Overweight salespeople in suits, would be more appealing if they were thinner. If you are overweight stop eating junk food, eat more grilled lean meat like chicken and fish, ad basic carbohydrates like salad veggies and/ or boiled and steamed veggies. Dump the bad carbs like potatoes, sugar, oil, white bread, pasta, white rice, fatty cheeses and soft drinks and other sugary drinks.

Have a balanced diet and limit the pasta and rice to a small amount in the afternoon to keep you going. Go to the gym and work out. You must be appropriate to the situation. You must be all things to all people, be able to communicate on all levels, one day you might be selling to a doctor the next day a truck driver who's every second word is FUCK. But most of all, you must look good.

For example...

If you went into the Doctor's office and you saw a man in blue overalls in the office you would think you were looking at the doctors mechanic, and furthermore if the man insisted he was the doctor you probably would have trouble believing him. The same way if you met a man in an expensive suit with a briefcase, and he told you he was a butcher. Now imagine you're at a party and you meet two men. Both are quite friendly and approachable. You find out that both are lawyers and you happen to have a small legal problem. One of the men is wearing a suit and the other a pair of jeans. Which one would you approach? To illustrate further, here's an old joke.

What do you call a biker in a suit? The defendant.

I know of Bikers that are professionals during the week but on the weekend they don the leather and fire up the Harley. But I think you get the drift.

Dress like your prospects demographic.

Tone

Rate of speech- It's important to copy or mimic your client, prospect or customer in speak and gesture. The only exception to this rule is obvious, and that is if your contact has a speech problem, like a lisp or slur or a nervous tick or other disability. But certainly, keep the pace.

Volume- Copy your customer, don't be too soft or yelling at him.

Pitch- I think you know this one.

Articulation- Or the way you put your words together, people that talk fast and use a lot of big words usually come across as a smart or more intelligent person, fine, as most of you are. By all means match with your client but don't use the big words on the person who might not be as smart as you, if you want to sell them. Remember you are to build rapport, emulate the way they communicate with you.

Verbal

What you're actually saying- usually you will find that your customer, if they are not objecting is still not hearing a lot of what you are saying, he likes you and is watching your moves. You will find that he may ask you something you have already explained. So the best thing to do is to paint a picture. "Just imagine, driving around in this baby with the top down, and the sun pouring in. The wind in your hair and the radio on, the light shining up that electric blue paintwork. Isn't she a beauty!"

1. **Disturb.**

If your cold calling this will happen anyway, if you are not , but are a competitor of a necessary product, for example, if you were a noodle supplier to Asian Cuisine Restaurants. Ask them to imagine what would happen if they couldn't get noodles. Try to create a fear or a distraction. If your teleselling the try not to say...

"Hi I'm Mary from Company XYZ printing, may I speak to the person in charge of your stationery purchasing?"

Because 9 times out of 10 the person on the other end will tell you that they are happy with their current printer and you can promptly get stuffed. When I was in the auto parts business we would get this all day long. I came to the conclusion long ago that 90% of salespeople were totally useless at selling!

Try having a joke or getting them off guard by creating a relationship that they think already exists like…

"Hi its Mary from XYZ here is Jack in?" Or "Hi its Mary from XYZ Printers, I've replaced Judy, She was last to speak to someone about your printing, do you know who that is?"

Use the same line when you get to the right person but first confirm that they are the right people that you want.

Never dismiss the receptionist as sometimes they can help you sell to the right person.

2. **Relax.** When you get to the right person use your charm after the disturbance, create the relief.

3. **Show the product.** This could mean explaining a service if you're representing an accountant or dentist, or an auto shop. But remember, paint a picture just look at a Coca Cola ad, when you want inspiration, people having fun in the sun, laughing and looking fit! Explain to your customer how he or she is going to feel, look, enjoy, save money, time, make money, make time etcetera, with your product or service.

4. **Features, Benefits and trial close.** Explain features and benefits. A feature is that "This car comes in metallic blue pearl." The benefit is that "it is tough, less likely to fade, and won't show the dirt as much as other colours." Trial closes are one-ended questions like "This car comes in metallic blue Pearl. It is tough, less likely to fade, and won't show the dirt as much as other colours, isn't that great?" **one ended questions are a trial close** you get the prospect to admit it's a good thing. Now let's rephrase the question.

1. Open closed and one ended questions

"This car comes in metallic blue Pearl. It is tough, less likely to fade, and won't show the dirt as much as other colours, do you think that's a great idea?" **closed question**

" This car comes in metallic blue Pearl. It is tough, less likely to fade, and won't show the dirt as much as other colours, what do you think of that?" **open question**

So what's the difference (Ok I know you have a bachelor of Arts majoring in communication but you didn't write the book did you?).

IMPORTANT
You must find out what your customer likes the most from your product. 99% of customers will like you because your service is cheaper than the one they have, but the rich guy won't care. So you have to find out why he wants it. A lot of large companies these days go for both ends of the market. For example, one soap powder company advertised whiter fresher clothes, with half the amount of most powders in cold water. They sold it for $14.50 per kilo. They also made another company and serviced the no-name side, and sold the same stuff in a different box for $3.99. This is where the company wins both customers and gets a better market share. I try to address Quality, Service and Price.

Or it lasts longer, If you need to know anything about it, or you need it fixed we are open 24 hours a day. It's also cheaper than everyone else. Or more effectively, Quality, Features, Benefits, Service, Value, Price.

The primal reasons people buy are to fill 5 basic instincts *hunger, sex, prestige, comfort, convenience.*

If your product appeals to more than 3 you nearly can't lose, provided they can afford it!

Remember you are also a product. You have to sell YOU, before IT! So go to the gym, hair stylist and dress nice. Dress to suit your customer (Don't wear an Armani suit if your selling lawn mowing services, except if the house is worth more than a few million).

People will buy because…

1. *It's bigger/ smaller.* A better TV has a nice big screen, or a prestige car is bigger. A mobile phone or laptop computer is smaller and lighter to carry.

2. *It's faster.* A computer can save time if it's a faster one.

3. *The colour is better.* I ♥ Samsung Phones.

4. *It's Cheaper/ it's more expensive.* Sometimes Cheaper is not always better, People don't buy Rolex Watches and Rolls Royce Motor cars because they are cheap. Now a Rolex will tell the time just like any other watch, but the basic model will cost you $6000.00
People buy a Rolex so that people that can't afford them, get jealous of a status symbol. Better Appliances, Like Grundig TV and HI-FI, Alpine car HI-FI, Westinghouse refrigerators all bring a higher price than standard stuff because they will last longer and are more reliable.

5. ***They will get treated better.*** Going to a five-star hotel where you are treated like a movie star, may cost more but hey Its worth it! Some companies don't offer good service, or they overcharge, and make mistakes. It's easy to be better than these companies.

6. ***It tastes, looks, feels, smells, sounds, better.*** "The burgers are better at Hungry Jacks" The slogan hails. You might buy a new car because of its shape. A new suit might be more comfortable. A new perfume or aftershave, even a new house in the country can smell better. Hi-Fi Systems like a *BOSE* might sound better. Even a better deal can sound better!

7. ***It makes you thinner, prettier, sexier, and fitter.*** Going to the gym, eating at a healthy restaurant, a new exercise gadget.

8. ***It's built stronger.*** BMW's and Volvo's are 'safer' cars because they are built stronger.

9. ***It's more effective.*** Better headache pills.

10. ***It's reliable.*** If you were going on a camping trip to the South Pole a tent bought at the supermarket on special might not cut it.

11. ***It's more advanced.*** Some people just like having the latest gadget.

12. ***It saves time.*** Dishwashers, Mobile phones, electric toothbrushes, electric shavers are all time-saving devices.

13. *It's more entertaining.* Films in the latest **W I D E S C R E E N** better to watch a movie at home.

14. *It has more than one of the above.* Bigger better faster more...

5. <u>**Disturb and relax.**</u> *Closed questions* put your prospect in a tense position they start with could you, would you, can you, do you? These types of questions work best with Dominant types, or analytical types *Open Questions* put your prospect at ease and relax them, they start with which, why, how, what and when. These types of questions invoke a conversational response and work best with **quiet and expressive types.**

We will go into character type later on

6. <u>**High Perceived Value.**</u> Art is worth what anyone is willing to pay for it. Some people would disagree with the price of art, especially the abstracts. But if everyone sells their Widget for $150, mine is worth $190 because it does it better and goes faster and comes in red, but you know what! because I want your business you can have it for $110, Now THAT sounds great doesn't it?

7. **<u>Relax them with a discount & trial close.</u>** So everyone hates to part with money. So I'm not going to charge you for the full $190 because, this week it's on special, it's only $110, now that's cheap isn't it? (well let's face it if this product or service gets a repeat customer your better off than having a high price and no customers. Now I don't mean you have to sell your stuff cheaper than everybody else, just enhance its value, make it appear better than the rest, and make it look expensive before you discount it for the price you want. In America one beer company was selling an average amount of beer, so in the TV ads they explained how they made the stuff, how much care went into it. Now the average selling beer became a great selling beer, even at a premium price. Now the fact is every beer company makes their beer that way. The trick is it sounded better.

9. Throw in a bonus and close.

As you already know, I like to keep fit I used to buy my supplements from the health food shops, but asking a little old fat lady about which protein powder is going to build the most muscle and help you shed fat, is like asking an Eskimo how to surf. Anyway, I was doing some sales work in Kensington an inner-city suburb 15 mins from Sydney. I happened across a bodybuilding shop, so I called in to have a look. The guy behind the desk asked me if I wanted some help. I said I have been working out for years but I can never seem to get rid of my belly. He said Hi my name is Joe and a lot of people have your problem, so here is a copy of the bodybuilder's diet, the one that the professionals follow. It's yours for free. So we talked for a while and he said I know you are going to stick to that diet so here is a free baseball cap with the shop's name on it. I was blown away! I had walked into this shop and as yet bought nothing and I got a free cap! Not only a cap but the best advice I had ever got. And you know what? This bodybuilding shop is an hour's drive from where I live, but I will never shop anywhere else. If I move interstate I will mail order off Joe, Because he is the best, and it's got a hell of a lot to do with the free cap!

Chapter 4 - Be easy to deal with

I can't remember how many times I've called a government office or a major bank and got put on hold for hours, or stuffed around by a computer menu. One major company in Australia was the only company for a particular essential service because they were the only ones doing what they did, they thought they could give crap service, they were even sometimes rude to the people that paid their wages. Then some competitors came along and put a big dint their customer base, and it was easy!

How many times have you (or your staff, if you are a team leader, manager or business owner) been involved in doing an important task and the phone rang and you had to answer it? Then did you treat the person on the other end like they were an interruption?

There is more to be said about this.
Have your phone number on the top of the website.
Quoting Richard Branson here, and you should read some of his books. If you start referring to your company as 'they' instead of 'us', the company has big problems. If staff or the team feel isolated and don't have a friendly rapport with the rest of the team in the company, that will subconsciously show.

So buy a copy of this book give it to your boss. Do so for a couple of reasons.

- Educate management as to what is actually involved in selling.

- For the management to understand the need and necessity of having a good working relationship, the support of the team behind the product, and behind the sales process. The company needs to deliver.

Here is a really good example of handling a negative situation

After signing up a customer for vending, a few weeks down the track I received a call at 7:30 p.m. with the manager telling me to get the machines out of there.

The problem was that the company had a lot of foreign workers, they were experiencing an intermittent problem with the vending machine but instead of actually calling up and speaking to our service technician using the phone number on the front of the machine they would just tell the manager. It wasn't long before the manager got the shits with this and he blew a fuse.
I explained to him that this is the first time that I have become aware of the problem, when a person uses the vending machine and then has a problem with it, they need to call up and explain what that problem is so that we can bring out the necessary tools or replacement part.
If we don't know about it we can't rectify it.
Everything calmed down and sorted out.
At the end of the year, I called in around Christmas time to bring around a bag of snacks and drinks as a thank you.
Often times customers have a problem and they just let it go because it's difficult to deal with and they have to make a phone call or send an email and just couldn't be bothered. The receptionist is the Gatekeeper if some other Vending Company shows up we need her on side. she needs to be the one that says we are happy with our current vending service we won't be changing.

When I called in to see the manager of the facility, he gave us more business. they had bought the lot next door and expand the manufacturing. After dealing with a small problem with the receptionist the manager overheard how I had dealt with the situation.

Jo, the receptionist said to me, "oh you are the vending company, by the way, I have purchased some of those yoghurt slices, two times they have been stuck, I believe that they are not heavy enough to fall through all the way, I wonder if there is a similar but better product?"

I explained to her, " it concerns me that you've had this experience and I'd like to rectify that immediately"
I opened my wallet and handed her $10.

Jo's response was " $10 dollars is too much money"

" It doesn't matter about the $10, I don't want any change, I want to walk away with you having a great day, and an awesome customer experience by turning a negative into a positive, please email my boss, and myself so that we can get our team to rectify problem and please take this cookie and see if you like it as a suitable replacement"
Jo thanked me, but was then concerned that I gave her my last $10.
"Jo, please don't be concerned about my $10, I have a credit card to buy lunch, and right now your happiness is the number 1 priority. The boss is likely to be shouting me lunch on Friday and I'm sure it will be rectified then so please don't be concerned"

10 very important statistics on sales.

- It is easier to sell to an existing customer than a new one.

- It takes 6 times more effort to gain a new customer.

- Only 4% of new cold calls say yes on the first call. (mostly).

- 30% of appointments will say yes.

- 90% of new customers will ring someone else if the phone won't answer.

- 40% of regular customers will try someone else if they can't contact you after 5 attempts.

- Your average repeat customer will last you for about 4 years, a good one, 6 years.

- 75% of new businesses fail in the first five years.

- 50% of the remaining ones will fail in the next 2 years.

- A customer will have to deal with you 5 times before they trust you and won't stray.

- A bad experience can result in the customer telling 11 people.

- A really good experience might have them telling only three.

With the odds against you like that, you want to love every one of your customers, even though some can be troublesome at times.

Business is more competitive today than it's ever been! To succeed, you have to know how to market effectively.

Unfortunately, most businesses have no idea how to get the most out of every marketing "dollar" spent. Many will just advertise anywhere and the fact is that most of the advertising rep or salespeople that place and take the ads for the phone books, and newspapers are only experts at selling to others and not helping them construct great ads. When it comes to the Internet most business even the big ones with a marketing department can stuff up a website.

The Top ~~Ten~~ Eleven Marketing Mistakes

1. You fail to keep your customers & prospects names and email addresses on a database

This is the simplest mistake to make and the easiest to correct. Your mailing list or customer database is your biggest source of lifetime profits!

To make your customer list really profitable, plan on contacting each person at least once a month even if your excuse is in the form of a newsletter, this is a personal way to keep in contact with them. These days with a computer it's easy to generate a personally addressed form letter.

2. Failing to up-sell a customer

Your hottest prospect is someone that has just bought from you. This is your best opportunity for another immediate sell. The key to successfully doing this is having products that offer solutions to the problems that your prospects have. Related problems and related solutions equals increased opportunity for sales.

Your job isn't over once you've sold your customers their first product. Just remember: your customers are never "hotter" than when they first buy or order something (do you want fries with that?)

You should look for a logical product or service to offer your customers. Using the back-end will turn one-shot sales into repeat customers. Great salespeople do it consistently.

3. Failing to follow up customers enough

You must commit to connecting with your prospects a minimum of 8 times. You need to contact your prospect time and time again and hit them with the same benefits and features over and over again until they take action you will usually have them by visit number eight if you're really bad at sales.

Set up a follow-up routine for yourself. Try to put them in a computer database with a form letter that prints out important details like a customer number, contact name, addresses, phone number, how and when is best to call in or phone. Print them out by postcode and put them in a file called **not contacted.** After you call them and get an appointment move them to your travel book or **display book,** (I'll show you how to make one of these later) if you don't get an appointment, file them in **'contacted, need to follow up'.** Customers that you have seen and didn't close go into a file called **'in the pipeline' (AKA Sales funnel).** You can expand this into manilla folders by postcode and date, if your not using CRM (Customer Relationship Management) Software. Every week or 2 go through your files and follow up your warm prospects. The customers you close, file them into your customer Database and don't forget to see them once in a while if you want to keep them or up-sell to them. If it's not your company, talk to your boss about a follow-up pay structure if you are on a commission basis.

4. Failure To Determine Specifically Who Your Target Market Is

Do you know who buys your product? Do you know how to cater and tailor your product or service to fit them better? A large percentage of businesses rarely make the attempt to determine who their market is, and what their market's desires, needs, wants, and passions are.

The successful online (Internet) business can tell you precisely who they're marketing to, and what their prospects and customers want in a product or service.

5. The facts you need to know:
 Why does your customer buy from you? What do your customers want or need most in the products or services you offer? How old are they? What do they eat, drink, do on the weekend?

Once you know the answers to these questions, you can focus your marketing efforts to show your prospects that you can satisfy their needs and desires. Most Internet companies read a file on your computer called a **cookie file**. The cookie file gets info added to it when you visit the commercial website, others read the file and learn what you like to do and your interests (don't worry you can turn this off if you like your privacy in your web browser settings)

6. IF you don't advertise and market, you won't sell zip

Even if you have the greatest product in the world you will never sell anything if you don't tell anyone about it. Without advertising, there will be no prospects, and without prospects, there will be no sales. It sounds like common sense, but it's also a common mistake.

You only have to do two things to be successful in business, and you only need to do one of them on a regular basis. Can you guess what it is?

8.You don't know how to write a sales letter that will get your customers to spend, or get them back to use you again.

If your computer was having a problem, and you knew NOTHING about computers (except where the USB goes) would you open the box and try to fix it? NO!

Your investment in a good copywriter will be worth more than anything else you'll ever spend your marketing $$$ on.

9.After-sales time

The worst thing a salesperson can do is not spending time after the customer commits. Don't just get up and leave. This customer just took your trust and became your friend don't damage the relationship.

10. Not contacting old customers that have been a little quiet

Customers can drift away. Don't take them for granted. Pop by and treat them like old friends. If your best friend has a store near you would you go anywhere else?

11. Not having a website

These days your company must have a website, keep your customers up to date with your latest products, even an online shop is a good idea. If you don't, your opposition might.

The Internet

Make sure that customers can get to you easy, these days we have the Internet. Companies like amazon.com started as a second-hand bookshop turned into a multinational online company nearly overnight. Why because they are easy to deal with, you can call, email, pay via any way you want. The products are delivered promptly. What started as second-hand books became, new books, then videos, and now just about anything. Companies can now deliver cheaply to your doorstep anywhere in the world. The problem is that a lot of companies that put themselves on the internet think that it only works in the company of origin. Companies that offer some kind of information service that thinks that there is only one country in the world. A little while ago I was selling stuff on an Internet auction called ebay.com, which I might add is a fantastic company. I was getting rid of some stuff in my garage. One man's trash is another's treasure. So I decided to run a search for some other auction sites. As there is almost no restriction in being able to send things overseas, well eBay does it. I tried to register with some others, some only worked in the US. HOW NARROW-MINDED! But you know what? eBay is the biggest online auction in the world and a lot of others have come and gone. Just remember that if you put your company on the Internet be ready for inquiries for all over the world! (subject to your Google ads Campaign).

Now 5 things you should never do with E-Business

- **Trashing your site with too many graphics, animations or annoying music.**

This has got to be the worst thing you could do to get rid of your customers. If you are running a business online, your web site's job is to inform and sell. Anything that detracts from this process should be avoided. One of the major cinemas in New South Wales in Australia, had a fantastic website that told you what was on and where and what time. Then they spruced it up with java and flash movies that made it near impossible to find out what was on. I found myself going to another cinema's website and therefore another cinema to see the movie I wanted. In summary, don't clutter it with things that take hours to load. The Internet is supposed to save you time.

- **Not making sure your website is focused on your customers and product.**

How many times have you been to a webpage for information on a product, and you couldn't find what you wanted because of all the other stuff there? Are most of the sites telling you what benefits you get if you become a customer? Or are they telling you about their company, how wonderful they are, what they do, how great their quality is, how many 'hits' they get, how great their service is, and all about them?

- **Having a web address like**

  http://www.coolwebsinc.com/~mypage/inde/widgets/home.htm

Come on. It costs about $80 US for a domain link www.widgets.com

- **Spamming or E-junk mail**

This is a pet peeve, you log on to get an important email from overseas and instead, you get 30 messages from people you don't know about the stuff you don't want. It is the biggest mistake that anyone (new or old to the Internet) can make. The common name for it is: 'Spamming'. There is no better way to run your online business into the ground than the act of sending unsolicited emails. A big mistake! I get everything from 20 companies telling me how to take online credit cards, MLM Business, wrinkle cream, chain letters. Imagine a good-looking guy like me, I don't need wrinkle cream! And I don't need a loan from the USA since I live in Australia!

- **Not working with your email**

These days customers are more likely to log on and use the Internet to buy your product or to find out more about you. This is because customers don't want to be put on hold, they want a solution. Your email communication with customers can make or break you. Give them the best service you can since most of the time you will never get a chance to impress them in person, you really need to learn how to use email to your advantage. Put a contact form on your website.

When you respond to an inquiry from your website, and/ or when emailing the prospect some more information, make a graphic up with your Client List and the biggest names and logos.
This gives you some validation and credibility.

Access and identity

Can customers get into your shop easy? Does it have an identity? Look at Mc Donald's they have a theme that runs through every store, advertising, staff uniforms, cars and trucks. Pick the colours for your shop and the layout and logos, and put it on your work clothes, cars, business cards and your website. It usually won't take much to get the look you want, whether it be a modern theme or a more traditional look, keep it uniform.

Chapter 5 - Closing

Closing, Getting rid of the... No goods **NG,** Knock backs– **KB,** Call backs -**CB,** Fails -**F**

Rephrasing questions and saying the right stuff so things go your way.

When should I see you? - Would Monday or Tuesday suit you best?

What time is the best? – Would AM or PM be best?

What colour do you want- Do you think blue is the best or perhaps orange or red?

The knock-backs.

If a customer tries to shut you down fast, " I can understand how you feel other people in the area have felt like that too, but after they have found how this vacuum cleaner can actually improve your health they became customers."

Getting the customer to close after you present to them.

This can sometimes be the hardest thing to do. They sit there nodding their heads, smiling and then you say and "that's all there is to it" and then they say, "OK, I'll give you a call" Bloody hell! You want to just choke them.

So here is a couple more aces up your sleeve. After you turn the last page in your display book and have trial closed them 5 times by getting them to nod and say yes when you say, "That's good isn't it?" quickly grab your contract, stick it under their nose and say "just put your autograph here and it's all yours." Or "how do you normally fix things up?" or " will that be cash or card?" "Delivery is Friday or Monday, Which day is best for you?"

Trial closing is very important

After every feature and benefit, you mention, get them affirming and nodding that what you have is good. "…and it comes in red, blue and metallic bronze, that's great isn't it?" " Pretty good eh?" "That's fantastic don't you think?" "You like that don't you?"

If they are nodding and saying yes throughout the tail end of your presentation, you know that the magic is working.

The no good

You get to the end and you say "just sign here" and they say "I'll have to get back to you." You now have a right to ask why, don't just say OK. Find out why. The response is usually…

1. I have to see my wife/ husband/ boss/colleague.

2. I need to think about it.

3. I don't have the finances right now.

These answers are commonly known as 'objections' in sales speak.

This goes back to what you are selling, if its door to door stuff, you should be able to close them, Now!

If you are cold calling companies (which you should ring first, and warm-up) the odds are that you will only close 4% so don't push it unless it's a low-value sale. So the value of the product/service or potential as a client has to play a part. If you can't close someone on the spot for an item under $100 then forget about them. They won't make up their mind anyway.

The main causes for someone not making a decision are the fact that customers lie.

- Prospect really didn't want what you are flogging anyway.

- You haven't explained the features and benefits in-depth or with enough enthusiasm.

- You started with the features and benefits instead of creating rapport and asking the right questions.

1. Having to ask someone else. " Does the husband/ wife/ boss make every decision? (Now this depends on the item service your selling and if you really do have the right person). I was told a story about how a disgruntled employee in a position of power signed contracts with a whole bunch of services in order to create problems the company hated working for. Sometimes the legal team need to look over the paperwork. If that's the case, try to make your paperwork very simple if you're finding it is a problem then talk to the bosses in making the paperwork in plain English and easy to read.

If you are selling female clothes… "you dress yourself in the morning don't you?"

Vacuum cleaners… " You are the one that does the vacuuming, or you can see the great advantages of having a machine like this…"

If selling a service to a company, it is usually the purchase officers decision, if it is a service to the staff, it would be the personnel manager.

" I thought you were the *personnel* manager, surely you are the one to make this decision?"

Putting the ball back into the court of the person you are dealing with, and make them (without being too obvious) feel like they have just told you that they are inadequate, haven't they? They don't have the balls to make a decision when the last five of your customers committed on the spot. *A better rule of thumb is to explain to the person on the phone when making the appointment that you will need both decision-makers to be present during your presentation*, if they don't agree to this and say "I'll take a look and explain it to the person who signs off" explain to them that you have a really busy schedule and what you're doing is very unique and highly in demand. You really don't want to waste your time with tyre kickers anyway.

2. Needing to think about it (if this is a low-value sale then this might be the first or second visit. If High value it may be number 6 visit that wins the deal).

Did I miss something? I have explained to you all you need to know about it to make a decision now, a smart person like you can make a decision now.

"You're a smart guy, everything you need to know we have discussed, if there's anything you're not clear on please tell me about it now so you can make a more informed decision if everything is clear then there would be no reason not to move forward, don't you agree?"

If they throw it back to you and say something like. "Well if I have to decide now the answer is no."

Chances are they really have said no. Give them your card, and say if you change your mind call me. Then get their number and you may want to call them another day, however, the chances are it will still be no.

When I was cold selling small low-value items (under $200), even If I had them over the moon with whatever it was, if they then said I have to think about it, if I had no luck all day, I would leave them a brochure and call back or ring them. It was better just to show up rather than telephone them. Calling them on the phone ended in no 99.9% of the time. Showing up without a prior call closed the deal 2% of the time. Worse odds than the original cold call. Whether you ring or show up, always take them back to how they felt at the time. For example, "Hi, Remember ME? Do you recall the way I showed you how you can save money with...

Do you remember how we talked about these fantastic features?"

You get the idea.

Sometimes you have them just not committing, They say "It all looks good, but we have to compare your offer to our current supplier." Or they just won't commit. This requires a bit more cunning. My favourite is the newspaper, email or post. Using a computer, scan the top of the newspaper and change the date to the future, make your contact the star of the paper. See sample (for ongoing service business or hi priced item).

Shares & Productivity up 150%
Val Morgan Hires Guy Glas

The **ASX Hit an all time high** on Friday when **Val Morgan** Agreed to Take on **Guy Glas as the Direct Sale's Exec for the Central Coast**

A spokes person for the corporate giant **Samantha Digby** Said that the new Recruit was The best move of Her career " Now that we have a top Sales Exec, Management & staff are

Off the charts

over the moon, This means that we are making big Money now!"

Guy Glas Had been self employed as a Marketing and sales Guru and Free lance artist

"After several contracts had ended I was looking for some work in the paper" Guy Said

"I had to Basically create relationships and build business for Val Morgan Personally I find Sales and marketing a cinch, I get on with clients from all walks of

3. I don't have the finance right now. This one's up to you to figure out. When people lie, they usually lift at least an eyebrow, Check for other signs of negativity, like folded arms, frowning etc. If you feel that this is not the reason then say to them "That's really not the reason is it? Tell me what it is so I can answer the questions you might have." This may be because you haven't generated enough interest, or failed to explain something. This way you give them and excuse to give you the reason for it. The other reason may be that they really don't have the money right now. If you can get it on the same day or the next would be a good sign. Ask to come past tomorrow and pick it up. The only problem with that is that they can talk themselves out of it by then. Sometimes you may have to just keep going back, but again it comes down to the value of the product and especially your commission. If it's an expensive item the company you work for should offer finance. You will then have to sell them the idea of finance. If you break it down over here it's only so many dollars/cents a week.

The Knock Back

This is where they shut you down pretty fast, and most of the time on a cold call. People are involved in something important most of the time. If they are at home they might be trying to wind down from work. The last thing they want is a salesperson to knock on the door. If you are in cold call sales you will know exactly what I mean. One way around this is to print up calling cards that let people know that you will be calling some time this week, from ABF Kitchenware to show them A NEW WAY TO COOK THAT'S FASTER AND MORE HEALTHY and leave them some FREE recipes (Demonstration takes 15 Mins and you are under no obligation).

I have found this has a better success rate than 'just calling' and even leads you to get in a house where you can present to them in the lounge room or kitchen table. This is harder for them to kick you out and allows you to slow down your presentation and build the relationship, 9 times out of 10 it will result in a sale.

Just on a note on presenting on the kitchen table, if you're presenting to a couple and they have kids it might be a good idea to take some colouring-in books. You want to distract those kids so you can get the attention of the couple 100% without constant interruptions.
The parents will appreciate your courtesy and mindfulness.

If your prospect is a company, the person you need to see may be having a bad day and just shut you down, this is where you may have to send a sample, a free gift or even flowers or chocolates. Send a card that says " I'm really sorry I upset you on the phone yesterday, I really can see a benefit for your company with our new widgets and how can I show you that if I can't see you, I want only 10 mins to see you and then if you don't like my widgets then I'll go." And leave your phone number on the bottom.

Knock backs are best to be avoided, rather than tackled head-on. This is done with what's called a good door opener.

Door Openers

1. Drop-in with free sample, and ask who the right person in charge is so you can give it to them (you may have to bribe the receptionist as well, and if it's a staff issue sell them on the idea too) or send the sample to the contact if you have them on file.

2. Send them one of those little teddy bears with a letter " bear with me for a   moment, there is a way for you to save money on your widgets, and I can show you in less than 10 minutes…" most women love a teddy bear, and they may have kids.

3. Call at different times if you keep getting their voicemail, like late at closing time or early in the morning, some times after 6 you will get them directly.

4. Hi, it's Guy Glas from Glas Enterprises my number is 029789 1234 a mutual friend asked me to give you a call about... (hang up) Most people will call you back. It's a case of "I just gotta know.'

5. Email some info to them before calling. If that fails, email some more stuff and call, or even post. They will eventually give in or have you arrested.

6. Intercom.
   Intercoms are pretty hard to get in to on a cold call, If you try, Hi I'm the Guy from XYZ Cable TV they will usually say thanks but no thanks. WHY? Because intercoms are usually attached to units in areas of high crime in high-density areas and usually the neighbours don't even talk to each other. So different things work in different areas. If it's a big building, try pushing a button at random on the 6th floor and say "Hi its Steve here from Number 102 you're the only person I got home, I've left my keys in the door can you buzz me in?"

Or "Hi this is Steve from XYZ Cable, and you have been randomly selected to qualify for a FREE demonstration of our new cable TV service, I need to see everybody at home so when is the best time to make an appointment to see you? 8 pm tonight? or would tomorrow be better?" or " Hi it's Steve from XYZ Cable, You Have just won a FREE Gift! Isn't that fantastic? To get the gift you have to (sign for it /Qualify), may I come up now?" When you get up to them show them your presentation. Drop calling cards in the letterboxes a couple of days before you call in and 'Warm Up' the area.

Back in the 80s the methods Encyclopedia Britannica would use would be to flier drop an area with a little quiz to win the Encyclopedia. These days with everything online their business model is defunct however this idea could work for something else. The method was quite clever at least you know that your prospect actually wants an Encyclopedia. People would fill out the form and post it to head office hoping to win. The salesperson would call them and say unfortunately you have not won the encyclopedia but you have a won second prize and I would like to pop around and hand deliver it to you.

 The salesperson would then offer you a free demonstration, they would roll out an actual size print out of how big the encyclopedia is and tell you how fantastic it is and talk about your child's education and the advantages of having an Encyclopedia, then they would tell you that it would only cost you $10 a week and you could pay it off.

BAM SALE!

Call back. Always try to give all the information they need, (keep a few bonuses up your sleeve that you can come back with if need be) make sure that you have the decision-maker or group in attendance (Husband and wife) (HR department head and social club secretary) so they can make a decision now. Use the formula and trial close. (Yes ladder, aka tie down statements).

Chapter 6 - The type of sales and how to perfect them.

When you know the odds you won't be so hard on yourself. Don't kid yourself, sales can be tough, and disheartening. Knowing that it's really a numbers game will help you to get the sales and measure your success. For example, if you Phone 20 Prospects you might get 5 that were not available, and 5 rejections. 10 may become appointments for the next day 2 will close straight away when you see them, 3 may never buy, and the rest may take some time. I know I have had to hassle some customers up to 20 times with a free service before I got a signature on a contract.

The cold call-Yes the nastiest of all, Let's start with house calls. First of all you knock on the door, and the door opens. Introduce yourself and try to match the person with the way you speak and move. " Hi I'm Steve from Lynx cable TV, How are you today?, That's a nice car you have Sir how long have you had that?"

The reason for this is that you have disturbed the guy, now try to put him at ease with a smile and before he can say NO THANKS! And shut the door, you have to show him that you are interested in him.

One time I was trying to find something nice to say about a house when the car was a heap and the house was run down and the garden was non-existent. But when the overweight middle-aged man opened the door I saw bookcases and rows of books The first thing I said was "Hello sir, I can see you're a reader, and books are a sign of a well educated and very intellectual and powerful mind!" The guy loved me! Ok back to the script…

"I always wanted a car like that, that's great, anyway I'm here from Lynx Cable, and we are here to explain some technological changes in your street / building (is better than.. doing a special promotion on a great new cable service), but it only takes a minute and is best shown on your kitchen/coffee table.

It's always good to look overloaded with a bag or display folder with papers sticking out. Its harder to say no when someone is inside your house. Now note that in intercity areas, you will have trouble with this kind of line. As people will be very security conscience, and may not even answer the door. If they don't answer the door, you could leave a brochure under the door but you will probably have to go back, and when they ask whom it is, explain that you are coming back to explain the brochure and answer any questions. If they don't open the screen door hold out a brochure near the handle, and when they open the door help it open and say "That's better you can see me now, as I was saying"...

Now get around the door and be careful not to invade personal space or you will blow the sale. Using your display folder or a brochure (whether you are inside or not. If you are inside, you can slow your presentation and make your prospect more at ease). "You might have seen the technicians last week installing everyone's service, and because Lynx Cable TV pride ourselves on excellent service, We thought that it's best to come around in person and show you exactly what it's all about." *Here you have disturbed and relaxed.* "What we have done is lay some new cables in your street, and because we want you as a customer we are doing something you are just going to love! So may I ask you when you watch TV, what **do you like to watch?**"

"Well, I like to watch **old sci-fi** movies and some offbeat stuff?"

"Well on Channel 8, we **have Star Trek** the original series, and on Channel 5 the movie classic channel we have screening 'A Clockwork Orange, Revenge Of The killer Tomatoes, Taxi Driver, and The Cook the Thief the Wife and Her Lover' and on Channel 3 **we have got all the Alien Movies, Stargate and Tank Girl.** All presented in **either widescreen** or standard, though only the **highest quality digital cable in 7.1 Sound**. That's good isn't it?" " Here is our TV guide, which normally costs $2 we will provide it to you free of charge for becoming a new customers. Just look at this, two **Music channels** 24 hours a day, two Sports channels, one extreme sport channel, the homemakers channel, five movie channels, three news channels and 24-hour cartoons.

"You would have to agree that this is a fantastic deal? So after a bad day at work, you can come home and relax with a beer and watch Star Trek. You would *have* to love that!" *The customer should have his chequebook ready by now!* Now normally the deluxe package costs $100 to install (optic cable is expensive) and the service would be $50 per month, but because we want your business, if you say yes now we will **install it for free** and your only charge is $5 per week! I can have a technician **out in 2 days and installation takes half an hour**, then sit back, put your feet up and enjoy crystal clear pictures for less than a video hire."

Now before he says I'll have to think about it, have your contract ready and say "this is number 12 and your name is... now just sign here."

Don't forget to spend a further 5-10 Mins and thank the customer for his business and leave him with the companies details and copies of all relevant documents.

Business call- If you cold call a business, there is only a 1% chance of closing the first time, Telephone them first and the odds jump to 45%. Give them a gift straight away. I find that this is a great icebreaker. Just remember if you are calling a business, you are probably interrupting something important. The prospect doesn't sit around all day waiting for a salesperson to swing past and jam something down their throat, that before you came along, they didn't want or need, and got along fine without it. That's why they MUST like you! Remember when Uncle and Aunt so and so came around they would always come bearing gifts. They were your favourites, weren't they? Perhaps you can give them a free sample, a company calendar, or other promotional stuff. It also helps if you know whom you have to see. Is it the purchase officer? The chief accountant? The personnel manager? Service manager? Logistic officer? etc. I usually look for someone in the car park and just say "hi, do you know whom I would see about widgets?" or at reception find out which person you would have to see. When you meet them, introduce yourself and your company. Break the ice with the gift and you might want to bribe the receptionist as well. Ask them can they spare 5mins. If they can't, make an appointment. If you can see your prospect, ask them "if there is somewhere we can talk."

Then using a display book, tablet, brochure or product sample, begin your presentation to them. (Remember communication is mostly visual). If you can't close them (usually because they have to see someone else about it) why not offer to meet with the whole group and assist in any questions that may arise.

<u>The phone call-</u> Telemarketing or Tele-Sales is tough work, Personally I think that the initial contact is made with the phone and an appointment is best made for the next day or two and treat it like you would a business call. Because you know they are expecting you, the sales pitch is a whole lot warmer.

When you ring up, suggest that the call is a warm call, If you are working from a database (a computer excel file that has been purchased from a marketing company) You should have the company contact person in your data. This is somewhat of an advantage. You can ring up and ask to speak straight to them. Or ask the receptionist if this is the right person for your product.

The receptionist is a trained Gatekeeper

Now there is a bit of psychology to phone sales, see the trick is to keep them guessing and make them laugh. They probably get 4 or more phone calls a day from salespeople, (most of which whom I might add haven't got a clue in how to sell). I know this as for the last 8 years I had a small company involved in making parts, we would get the same calls all day long.

"Hello, could I speak to the manager or the person who is in charge of your photocopier repairs?"

I would say "Oh he's out at the moment."

If you keep them occupied with the jokes and creating a relationship, you will keep their finger 'OFF' the KILL button. It's much easier to hang up on someone than to slam a door.

Example

" Hello, how are you, did you get your washing off the line it looks like rain?" *This usually will send the receptionist into hysterics (much better than "Hi, I am from a company called **Vend a drink** can I speak to the person who is in charge of the staff facilities?" The receptionist will probably shut you down in two seconds flat, you have disturbed her, but you didn't make her think. I can't believe the number of sales companies using this stupid spiel)*

The receptionist will respond with who is this? This is because the receptionist really usually intercepts calls for everyone else. Anyway you say "Oh sorry, my name is Kale from Venda Drink. Someone from my company was speaking to someone from your company and I get to sort the mess out, would you know who is in charge of you drink machines?" Oh before you put me through to them, do you know how much you are paying for a drink from the machine you have?" You can get a lot of information from a receptionist if you get them on side, Sometimes they will do the selling for you.

Now when you get to the right person you could even catch them off guard by saying, "My name is Kale from Venda Drink. Remember when I called you last month and you were too busy to see me, well I was wondering if I could swing past tomorrow and drop off that **FREE SAMPLE PACK?"**

This will usually get you in, Or " Hi John, My name is Kale from Venda Drink and you have just WON a bottle of fine red wine! but the catch is you have got to have a five minute meeting with me about how we can give you a better vending service, now what is the best time to call? In the AM or PM?"

OR

" Hello, how are you? Now I bet you are sitting there in air-conditioned comfort, aren't you? Do you know how hot it is today?" *The* receptionist will respond with who is this? "Oh sorry, my name is Kale from Venda Drink. Rumor has it that you have a coke machine, could this be true? How much are they charging you for drinks? $2.50 That's too much! Wouldn't it be great if they were only a$1.80? And you can get bigger sizes and 100% pure fruit juice, and 600ml bottled water, and Powerade and 415ml Pepsi for the same price? Well If you could help me out with the person in charge of that, you might just have earned yourself some free drinks!

A few years back, I did some contract work for a telemarketing company. With this particular job, I had to call pre-qualified people to download some rating software. The list was from a database company. The Company had a pre-qualified list picked, with people that...

1. Liked doing surveys and research

2. Had computers.

3. Had the Internet available on a Laptop or desktop.

The script went like..

(company names have been changed)

Hello <____>my name is GUY I am calling from XYZ net ratings, Australia's internet research company.

We produce an internet rating system similar to what IMDb do for TV ratings . . .

We don't do phone surveys . . . We advise the IT industry as to what Australian users really want from the internet.

When you currently use the Internet, is it more for work or personal use?

On a PC or Mac or Linux?

Great. We're currently seeking panelists from all walks of life to be a part of our Work User program. We're registering members all over Australia and the members are given all sorts of things to say thank you for being a part of the program – everything from free movie tickets to discounts and after 6 months you will also receive a $100 voucher for shops like XYZ designer clothes, XYZ big book store, ABC big record store or ABC big cosmetics firm.

It doesn't take any of your time. . . the panelists simply load some software onto their PCs and this acts as a counter to Australian websites they go to. It's not able to record passwords and sensitive data - it just gives us a cumulative figure across Australia of internet use . . . and we publish this information in places like The Financial Review, and the major state papers.

How does this sound to you, is it something you'd like to be a part of?

Great. What I can do for you is sent through an email that will have a link to our website.

This will tell you who we are and how it all works.

It's a very simple process to register online, it takes only a few minutes. You'll be asked to clarify your details at the beginning of the process . . . this is strictly for XYZ net ratings . . . it won't be given out to a third party. So, on the email I send you there will be a 1800 number you can call to have any questions answered.

What would be the best email address to send that through to?

<u>Take Details></u>

Great < > we will give you a quick call in the next day or so to make sure that the registration went smoothly and answer any questions you may have.

THANKS FOR BEING A PART OF THE PROGRAM!

Now, this script was fine. It scored a 5 out of 10 hit rate. By modifying it to… (Changes in bold)

Hello <___>my name is GUY I am calling from XYZ net ratings, Australia's BIGGEST Internet ratings company.

We would like your help and are willing to pay you.

We produce an internet ratings system similar to the ABC TV ratings . . .

We advise the IT industry, as to what Australian users really want from the Internet.

When you use the Internet is that on a Smartphone, PC, Mac, Chromebook, or Linux?

Fantastic. **We're currently seeking a very special unique team of 3000 members to be part of our elite panel. Not only are you being paid for the work, you would also receive gifts from our client and its partners. Everything from free movie tickets to discounts and after 6 months you will also receive vouchers for shops like XYZ designer clothes, XYZ big book store, or ABC big cosmetics firm and 100's of other goodies.**

It doesn't take any of your time. . . the panelists simply load some software onto their PC and this only counts Australian websites you visit and nothing else. We publish this information in places like The Financial Review. All the data is anonymous.

Now this scored a 9 out 10 hit rate. After some time the pre-qualified list ran out. So we started to use a list from the phone book. I called foreigners, 75-year-olds, the lot. With the above script the hit rate went to 1 out of 20. I went from earning $100 for 2.5 hours to $7 for the same amount of time. Even people that were qualified just blew me off. Since this was the main source of income for me, I got depressed and frustrated. This is bad news for the sales guy/ gal. If you keep getting the phone slammed down you want to say to hell with it. If this happens to you take a day off and re-focus.

Eventually, I had to rethink the whole script. The first 5 seconds of the call will make or break you. If I was going to earn less (paid per contact) the database had to be blasted through a lot faster.

The new script

"Hello < ___ > I am calling from XYZ net ratings.

This is NOT a Sales Call.

A few months back you had entered your information into a form online to earn some money from home.
Now who doesn't like free money? Our website rating software will earn you money when your computer is online you can turn it off and on at any time.

All I want to achieve tonight is to send you some information by email."

Now if you like I can explain what it's about or would you prefer for me to just send it?

Explanations

Have you heard of ABC TV ratings.? They pay specially selected people to watch TV the way they normally would. We produce an Internet ratings system similar to that but instead of installing a box on your PC we can do it with a small piece of software.

We have the software for both Mac and PC

Which one is best for you? Great.

We are only selecting 10 people from each major city to participate as an elite panel across Australia. In addition to money you will also receive gifts from our clients - everything from free movie tickets to discounts and you will also receive shopping vouchers etc.

This got me a hit rate of 8 out of 10. (This way I blazed through them)

Sales meeting _____

So you go in and meet the person you have to sell to. Introduce yourself and shake hands. These days women in business shake hands too but it's not the same as a man's handshake it's like the way you would put your hand forward to dance. If you are a male you would only shake a woman's hand on leaving and not on greeting.

You can pretty much ask anyone anything when you are walking together, this is a good time to take an interest in your prospect to ask them how long they have worked for this company, "is it a good job?" Share some general things about what you'd like to do on the weekend as long as it's not too weird, or you can tell a funny story. Talk about the latest film. When you sit down for your meeting if the person you are seeing is shorter than you sit down first. This shows that you are leaving them in power. Try to side at 90 degrees or near them, not across from them. Show them your display book/presentation or flier (people remember images before words). Then, go through the formula...

1. ***Make friends and create a relationship.***

Make sure you copy their gestures, don't forget to Smile.

Your disturb, creates a 'what's going on type situation' in the prospect's mind. Ask questions to find out what your customer's needs are.
What kind of budget range do you have for this type of project?

What would you like to see from a company like ours that you have not found to date?

Who else, other than you, of course, will be involved in or impacted by this decision?

How can I help you do your job better?

2. **Relief**

3. **Show what the product is.** Paint a picture. How will your customer use the product.

> The world's greatest hypnotists have their clients imagining themselves in a certain situation. The person is lead to 'lucid dream' to lose weight or give up smoking. Hypnotists use a thing called autosuggestion to test the subject's susceptibility.

> Try this with a friend. Ask them to stand up with their eyes shut. Tell them to "Imagine that they are standing across a plank of wood that is nailed across a small rowboat. The rowboat is in the middle of a pond. There are ducks in the pond and the sun is shimmering on the water. The wind rustles through the dark green reeds that line the shore etc. The wind causes the boat to rock gently from left to right, left to right. A gust of wind then blasts them in the chest."

Your friend should be swaying about by now. You can even tell him that he is falling backwards (stand behind and tell him you will catch him) "falling, the wind is blasting your chest, falling backwards, falling."

This will work on most people, don't worry if it doesn't, your friend just wants to show you that it won't work, if he catches on to what you are doing.

In the same way, create the image in your prospects mind to make them daydream about what you have. That's when they will buy it.

5. *Features* and ***benefits***

6. *Trial close*

7. *Disturb and relax*

8. *High perceived value*

9. *Relax them with a discount*

10. *Throw something in, get a commitment and put them over the moon!*

NLP - Neuro-linguistic programming.

It's just a fancy term for using words, that appeal to the subconscious, and bend the customer to your will. You want your subject to mentally engage with you're offering, to see themselves using it, to see themselves enjoying it's features and benefits.

There is a myth that a salesperson has 'the gift of the gab'. This is not entirely true. A good salesperson knows how to listen, and listen enough, that the client will pretty much sell the product to themselves. Your job is to direct the conversation. A good salesman knows how to create value, the features and benefits of products against the personal needs and wants, to bring them together to create value. You want to be sure when using the yes ladder, because you should never get yourself into a situation when you Test Close and there is a NO response from the prospect. You should even know if the client is on-board, or not, so do more work or back off. You want to be talking to the customer about the future, because we are going to be long-term business associates.

Smile, Smile, Smile! Put a smile in your voice, on your face and you will have money in your pocket. To put yourself and others at ease, and sooth defenses, smile. Your energy even on the phone, speaks much louder than words. That's how you instinctively know when the person on the other end of the line has stopped listening. If you are angry and saying "how nice" this comes across in your voice.

While on the subject of phones, put a mirror in front of you when you are on the phone selling so as to know what sort of image you are projecting "over the wires"

COPYCAT

The copy cat game helps you strike a chord and warms up rapport with other people.

Learn to march to the beat of someone else's drum. When you actively listen, breath, and emulate others, they become part of your team. Others will enjoy supporting you in your quest. Try to understand others and they will understand you.

Copy Words

Repeat back the words and phrases others use to express themselves. This lets them know that they are being heard and this allows you to step out of your shoes and into theirs. With this knowledge you will be better equipped to give them the solution to their needs. Active listening is the most single important thing in successful sales communication.

Ask someone something, listen to the answers and then restate his or her reply back to them. This proves to them that you have been listening and they have been heard, a critical factor in establishing rapport.

For example

You: "Why did you buy that car?"

Them: " It's nice and big and rides like a limousine."

You: "So you like a big car with a limousine smooth ride?"

Them: "Yes, that's right!" And they will love you for that.

Copy Breathe

Notice how the other person is breathing try to stay with their rhythm copy tone.

Speak and copy the other person's tone, rate, pitch and speed. Copy the time and pause between each word. If the other person is loud and fast. You are loud and fast. If the person is soft toned, copy.

Copy dress

If you are calling on corporate companies, wear a suit. If you are calling on houses, dress in smart casual. When in Rome, do as the Romans. If the other guy is wearing shorts and a T-shirt, you probably would be hard pressed relating to him. Try starting to dress like your bosses boss, when in the office and see what happens. As the saying goes dress for the job you want and not the job you have.

Copy Gesture

If they sit there with one leg crossed and their hand on one side of their face, mirror what they are doing. This will make them feel like they are your pal.

Remember peoples names

If you want to get on with someone you must remember his or her name. I remember going to a dinner one night. It was a business dinner, like a trade night. One guy (I don't think I ever meet before) came up to me and said "Hi Guy, How is the shop going? Have you still got that old car you are fixing up? This impressed me, I had obviously met this fellow before and he had known a lot about me. When I met him, I must **not** have thought him to be an important fellow to remember. Remembering my name made me feel like I was important to him and he probably would have got some free advice out of me, or a discounted job, you see I felt like I owed him something.

YOU are not important, YOU are a salesperson, YOU want me to part with money. Part with money to give you for something my life was fine without.

Watch what happens when you return call on a prospect and you say "Hello Steve, how was Golf last week?" and Steve Says "Oh Hi um How are you?" They may even ask you what your name is again. Or ask you for a business card. This is a neat trick if you forget them as well.

Another way you remember names is to get a picture in your head to associate the name and the face. Ever heard someone say that they remember faces more than names? For example his name is Mr. Adam Farmer. Remember Adam and Eve with fig leaves over their privates? So remember Adam Farmer stand there with a farmer's hat, pitch fork and a fig leave and gumboots just about nude. Or MRS Drinkwater drinking a glass of water. Garry Jones. Gary like scary and Jones Davy Jones locker under the sea. Think of him as a sea monster. Other people have outstanding features like a big nose or big ears that will help you remember them.

Chapter 7 - The 4 Personality Types and How to Sell to Each

1. Assertive

Assertive personality types are goal-oriented, decisive, and competitive. They care more about getting it done than creating relationships. They probably won't send you a Christmas card, but if you deliver on your promises, you'll maintain a healthy business relationship.
With assertive people it's all about the bottom line.

Assertive people want the information fast and they can be controlling but they just want to get the job done.

Assertive personality traits:

You are probably dealing with an assertive type if they come into a car yard and say "I am looking for a new 4x4 car?"
Rather than, "Can you show me what you have?"

Assertive types are more animated, and have a confident stature and tend to be 'forward'.

How to sell to them:

Be professional if you don't know something, let them know that you will get back to them. Don't give half correct answers.

Assertives appreciate efficiency. Don't waste their time, cut to the chase.

You should emphasize how your product or service will solve their problem, there is no point talking up the latest technology in fiddly detail, unless you can demonstrate why they will be useful to them or their company..

They have a competitive nature, you can use this to your advantage by showing how your product or service will give their business or them a personal advantage.

Many sales people talk about how the customers love the certain feature, with assertive types talk about how much money the customer your citing saved or how much return on investment. Avoid, personal opinions and testimonials.

When dealing with customers, I like to paint a picture with things like, "imagine you're in this situation, now really visualise it. This does not work so much with assertive people they tend to want to hear about how your product will solve a problem.

2. Amiable

This character type is the one that will assess what kind of person you are when you greet them, they like to build trust. They have a creative side and want you to tell them a story with imagery. They probably have not researched your product or your company beforehand, however, that will allow you to guide them to making a decision based on rapport and merit.

Unlike Assertives, amiable people don't make decisions quickly. You need to explain in detail the awesome technology, the features, the benefits... if you don't tick all of the mental boxes, the prospect may go away, and ask for a group decision. A lot of times I mention, when on the phone to the prospect, before the meeting, "are there any other decision makers that need to be present?"

Amiable personality traits:

Amiables are laid-back and informal, great listeners and might ask more personal questions in an attempt to get to know you outside of your professional role. They will be friendly, calm, and patient during meetings.

How to sell to them:

Pitch a vision. Help them visualize the outcomes their business could achieve with the help of your product or service.

Take time to build rapport. Amiables will need to feel safe in their relationship with your company before they'll be comfortable doing business with you.

I tried to throw in something for all personality types in my presentation. Bring up examples of similar clients who have successfully used your product. talk about the solutions you've provided to your other clients in the context of a story "so XYZ company are a client of ours and they had this issue with their provider of the ABC product, 9 times out of 10 it would be fine but when it became crucial to use it on a big job, this is when that problem would come up.
Try not to diss your opposition, however, in saying that I'm very guilty of it, especially if the prospect is already pissed at them, I will play on it, the other expert sales people will tell you this is a no no. Details like these are convincing for Amiables.

Take the role of an expert and walk them through the decision making process. Instead of overwhelming an amiable with information, help them through the process and act as an advisor.

This personality type will expect you to be personally responsible. It's good to back your brand and offer that hundred percent money back guarantee. If they are not entirely happy they can just cancel and you will make sure that that is taken care of for them. It will calm their anxieties and make them more likely to buy.

3. Expressive

Expressives are the personality that want to take care of the group, very important to this personality type.

Some people can be a mix of personalities, this trait however stands out. They will be concerned with the well-being of others, whether it's their employees or their customers, the expressive personality type will want to know how decisions they make affect the people around them. They tend to be people-pleasers, You want to get them on side and they will sell the idea to others if your views conflict with their views you won't come out a winner. They have powerful personalities and use them to convince others of their strongly held convictions.

Expressives are creative, outgoing, spontaneous, and rely on their intuition. They value mutual respect, loyalty, and friendship. Don't make offhand commitments to Expressives -- reneging on an offer could spell the end of your relationship.

Expressive personality traits:

Expressives tend to be very enthusiastic and colorful. Like Amiables, they'll want to bond with you and feel connected on a personal level, but like Assertives, Expressives are sure of their beliefs and speak more in statements rather than questions.

How to sell to them:

Present case studies. Expressives want to be reassured that you're looking out for them, and what better way to prove your track record than to show stories of how your business made an impact on other people's lives?

Emphasize building a relationship. If your company offers exceptional customer service or maintains long-term partnerships with its clients, explain all about it.

Don't focus too much on numbers and details. Data is important, but an Expressive will ultimately want to know how their buying decision affects their company in the big picture in a human way.

Go Back to what you've said summarise, using the less ladder and constant trial closing for nods, yes and smiles.

4. Analytic

Those with an analytical personality type, have done their research on you most likely before the meeting. They want to know the data and will look past the pretty story you tell them. You will know when you have one because you'll be hammered with all the technical details.

Analytics, don't always make a decision then and there, they might need time to Mull over the details. If you fail to close them on the spot, open your diary and ask them how many days they will need to make a decision and put a date in the diary to go back. Explain to them that there will probably be some final questions. The analytical type will stick to their decision once it is made, they also stick to their deadlines.

Analytic personality traits:

Analytics, are all about the numbers, they are less interested in building rapport and will spend little time in the getting to know your part.

How to sell to them:

Don't rush them, they will likely want to go away and research, what you have presented. If you're good you'll be able to get them on the next visit. They just need time to gather all the information before making a final decision. Never rush an Analytic.

As salespeople we tend to bend the truth a little bit try to avoid too much hype. The analytical type tend to see-through it.

Instead of saying this product will save money and has a longer life, provide an example of how much money it has saved 'Insert company name here', and how much more mileage they got out of it. They are happy to listen too much more information in detail than the other personality types and thank you for mentioning it.

If they come across as a bit cold don't try and force the friendliness as it will work against you, they will know if you are being buttery.

Just remember that most people are a mix of these personalities and won't necessarily fit in a singular box metaphorically speaking but once you're familiar with the types you are dealing with, you'll be able to bend your strategy to suit any situation that comes up.

Chapter 8 - The follow up

HOW TO PLACE SUCCESSFUL FOLLOW-UP PHONE CALLS

The success of your follow-up call is contingent on having a good previous call. And when you do call back, use these ideas, and you'll increase your chance of success.

DON'T ASSUME NEGATIVES

Speaking of negatives, too often sales reps assume the worst before a call, and then let that attitude come through in their voice on the call.

Their assumption becomes reality. Everything first manifests itself in the mind. For example,

"I know you're busy so I won't take too much of your time..."EVERYONE is busy. If what you have is of value, you earn their time, and they'll want to speak with you. "I imagine you get lots of stuff in the mail and probably

haven't had a chance to look at my material yet..." Instead, tell them that you are calling to review the material that you have sent them as a result of your previous call. If that call was strong, and they agreed to look at your material and do something with it, you should expect that on the follow-up call.

Many sales reps make the mistake of sending out literature after a brief prospecting telephone call, and begin the follow-up call with the "mail inspector" opening:

"Hi, I was checking to make sure you received the literature I sent."

Then they follow with the equally ineffective,

"Uh, do you have any questions?"

After hearing "No, no questions," they end with, "Well, keep us in mind if you ever need anything."

The listener, trying to sound as sincere as he can while lying (or suppressing laughter) responds, "Oh, OK, I will."

So why do most follow-up sales calls go nowhere? Two reasons:

1. The initial call was ineffective, therefore the follow-up is not much warmer than the first cold call.

2. The use of go-nowhere, rejection inducing approaches and questions on the follow-up.

Here are ways to correct both of these problems.

First, you need a good reason to follow up. Make your first call better.

Don't simply introduce yourself, say you'll send literature, and rush off the phone. That ensures a follow-up that's almost like another cold call. Be sure it's even worth your time to call back. Ensure the prospect will do something between the initial call and the scheduled follow-up. For example, they commit to checking your prices vs what they pay or testing the sample or demo you send.

As for the follow-up call tactics, the opening needs to bring them into a conversation that readdresses the hot points from the last call, and also moves the process closer to the ultimate action you seek (the close or appointment) Here's a simple format for the opening.

1. Introduce yourself. The easy part. Name and company will do: "Hi John, this is Guy Glas from Smith Brothers Software, how are you?" An even better process is to actually have them trying to think who you are.
If you have the direct number you could try.. " Hi John, how's life?" the typical responses, " Yeah not bad, who is this?"

You can act like you might be slightly offended that they have forgotten you.
" It's Guy" short pause to let them think "You know from so-and-so company, My boss asked me to call because you've been having some issues with your something software"

2. Bridge. Bring them back to where they were emotionally when you ended the previous call. Remind them of their interest.

"...I'm calling to pick up where we left off two weeks ago, where we went through the time and money you would save with the project management of your ..."

3. The Agenda for This Call. This part needs to be proactive: "I'd like to review the material I sent you and point out the cost-cutting features that apply specifically ..."

Other proactive words and phrases include, "discuss," "analyze," "cover," and "walk through."

Also, include a value-added reason for this call, this way if their interest has waned since the last contact and/or they didn't follow through with what they said they'd do (which happens quite often) you still have a basis for continuing this contact. For example, "And I also did some research and came up with a few other examples of something you showed interest in the last time we spoke: how other Building firms have used this process."

Chapter 9 - DON'T VALIDATE THEIR RESISTANCE

When a prospect or customer gives confrontation, don't put words in their mouth to validate the resistance. Make them do it themselves. For example, I heard this on a call: Prospect (tentatively): "So we probably won't be doing

this with you in the short term..."

Caller: "Oh, so you're really not in a position to do it now?"

Prospect "Yeah, ... right, we're really not in a position to do it now."

The rep then said, "Can I call you back in about three months?", and the prospect said sure.

And why not? The caller made it so easy! Instead, the rep should have remained silent after the initial resistance,

Since there might not have been much substance behind it. It's interesting how, when people aren't telling the complete truth, feel compelled to keep talking when confronted with silence. If the prospect didn't volunteer further information, the caller could have said, "Oh, what led to that conclusion?"

This way, the caller finds out if the prospect is serious, or is simply brushing off the caller.

Don't go into a call expecting resistance. If you must expect anything, expect success, and if you doubt anything, doubt your limitations.

You can't begin to sell until you are invited, and you need to get your prospect to agree to see you, so this usually starts with a letter, a phone call or a visit leaving some information, then perhaps a follow up email. What are you saying that communication makes a difference.

This process is called the sales funnel, you have to keep feeding it or the process dries up. To be invited you have to be appealing. You need to be able to say what you want in a way that is compelling and interesting. You need to plan what you're going to say in your sales copy, on your commercial paraphernalia, (sometimes known as collateral), fliers and business cards, sales letters, and pre-planning scripts for phone calls.

All this with your prospects already being bombarded with other companies offering other services and products constantly.
This is why you really need to stand out so much, that they are going to want to talk to you.
You need to see your business or product from the customers eyes. You need to create the first two sentences on the features and benefits of your product or service, something that your potential customer wants to see.

To the average person if you ask them what they do, they might tell you that they are a plumber, or an accountant.
Selling is when you can describe the benefit of your service or product through the customer's eyes.
A security guard may describe his work as "I do night time security patrols".
The security guard service sales rep would describe his job as "I help you to sleep at night so you can feel safe knowing that your business is protected with not only an alarm system but security people whom patrol your place of work during the evening, when burglars like to take advantage of the darkness."

If I tell you a story about how, I saw a dog running and jumping up on a person. 90% of people who just read that sentence visualised an image of a dog running and jumping on a person. The techniques I've chosen to teach in this book are NLP, neuro linguistic programming. This is known as a VAK statement, Visual, Auditory and Kinetic. In all of your marketing materials and your sales pitch you need to trigger this VAK phenomenon inside the prospects brain to achieve Maximum Impact. Some people learn things by watching videos, or seeing a demonstration, some people learn things by reading or listening, some people only learn things by practicing them. For most people it's a mix of all three, if you use this system, no one can escape your powers.

At the end of your sales letter, brochure, telephone call, you need something to happen, you need the prospect to take action. This is known as a call-to-action.
You have to decide what you want, it may be to book a more in depth phone call, it may be to book a meeting. It all depends on what your product or service is, to increase the likelihood of a solid deal it's best done in steps this gives you an opportunity to build rapport.
The first step is to sell you people talk to people, calling up and saying, " Hi this is John from ABC company, I have called you to ask you about who the decision-maker is in regards to your Information Technology Services."

This will trigger our response in the trained professional receptionist brain to immediately tell you that they are happy with whom they have and to promptly f*** off.

You have to stand out and break this pattern, one way to do it is to simply call up and sound like you're in a hurry "Hi I need to talk to Ken Smith, is he about".

Another way would be to use a third-party as a reason for the call.

" Hello, Super Fast Logistics this is Sue speaking how may I direct your call?"

"Hi Sue, the boss has asked me to give you a quick call, Our company is the very awesome dry cleaning service down the road. I was going through our records and I don't have a contact, I'm wondering if you can help me with that?"

The call has to be not a cold call, it has to be a call for a reason. When offering vending services I would call them up and say "I've got a free lunch for you, or I owe you a lunch and I'm paying." if I was selling nightclub services I would say, " I was there the other night and it looked like you needed a full dance floor, your venue has so much potential you just need the right person to bring the right noise and they will beat a path to your door."

Just a quick note, don't lie on your phone call, don't say things like, "I was looking at your records," if you don't actually have a record. "I went to your nightclub, it was empty." It may have been actually going off the hook. No one's going to do business with a liar, especially if you start your phone calls with lies.

A great way to start a call is, as an implied relationship. "My company looks after your neighbour company next door." Always engaged the prospect with a question. "How do you guys currently handle your *thingy me bobs?"*

or by using a referral, " I know that you know, Steve at *ABC company,* because you buy spare parts from him, we look after their *so- so service,* and Steve said that you guys would be really keen on *that thing* as well, your company used that yeah?"

Always make sure you have a call-to-action, "I've got this free sample of *that thing* that we do, I'd love to drop it over and show your purchase officer. I have Tuesday morning free or Wednesday afternoon, when is the best time?"

You need to personalize your script you need to take the formula above and put it in your words and treat it like a normal conversation. If a Sales Manager or business owner has handed you a script you need to put it in your words. There are many people that end up in positions of power not because they earned it, but because they knew somebody. I've had sales managers that were the bosses Son. I've worked for companies where the owner of the company used to do the selling and tend to think they knew everything. If you have one of those people above, it might be an idea to hand them a copy of one of Richard Branson's books.

Richard Branson is one of today's most successful entrepreneurs with his Virgin brand. He always says that the key to success is not micromanaging staff, but instead looking after them, and giving them a reasonable leash to try things. If the staff are happy they will look after their customers.

Direct Marketing with mail

How To Write Headlines That Will Attract Interested Prospects and Sell More of Your Products or Services.

I have used the VAK process in the above statement. Writing is Kinetic, people that are interested will listen to what you have to say (auditory) and see what you have to offer.

All your marketing materials must contain headlines if you want them to sell. Take a look, they are all through this book.

This includes all ads, sales letters, websites, press releases, etc. And yes, I did say websites. Some people don't realise that their website is an advertisement. I come across far too many websites that don't include a headline telling me why I should stay and browse the site! The headline is what gives your prospect a reason to read your ad (or another marketing piece). People don't just read what's put in front of them. They read what interests them and can benefit them in some way. This applies to websites too! With so many websites failing to use this basic, highly effective marketing tool, your site will stand out in the crowd with a compelling headline.

Why should all your marketing materials have headlines?

First, competition for your reader's attention is fierce. Every day, people are bombarded with the advertising of all sorts: TV and radio commercials, billboards all over town, newspaper and magazine ads, numerous forms of advertising on the Internet. Even shopping malls are overflowing with ads - special prices, new and improved products, low-fat this, and sugar-free that... and the list goes on.

People are becoming numb to this excessive exposure to advertising. If you want even the slightest chance of selling your product or service, you'd better have a powerful headline to grab their attention.

Next, you only have a split second to catch your prospects attention. If you don't have a headline that commands immediate attention, the rest of your copy goes unread. Which, of course, means you won't get the lead or make the sale.

Types of headlines

Here are some of the most common types of headlines you can use:

1) The promise of a major benefit

2) A solution to a problem

3) Flag headline

4) Warning headline

5) Testimonial headline

Often times, good headlines use a combination of these, and I'll discuss each of them in detail.

1) The promise of a Major Benefit

This is the safest, most widely used type of headline. And for it to be as effective as possible, it must display the #1 benefit your prospect will receive by purchasing your product or service.

The most effective way to determine this benefit is to survey your customers - by phone, email, or postal mail. Ask them the top 3 reasons for purchasing your product or service, and have them rank them in order. It's a good idea to offer your customers an incentive for providing you with this information. A free report related to your product or service is easy to write and will give you leverage in getting more responses. Once you get 10 (preferably 20 or more) responses, the #1 benefit will be clear. Then simply incorporate this benefit into your headline.

If you don't have any customers to survey, you may have to do the work yourself. Write every benefit a customer would experience with your product or service. If you really spend some time on this, you may be surprised to find that what you thought was the #1 benefit was actually secondary. List everything you can think of and don't hold back - a minor benefit may spark a new idea - revealing the most important benefit. This process can make the difference between an ad that flops and an ad that brings in record-breaking sales.

Once you have the #1 benefit, you're halfway there. Use some of the following techniques to craft a winning headline for maximum profits.

2) A solution to a problem

This type of headline is a slight variation of the #1 benefit headline. The problem solved by your product or service is the #1 benefit - it's just presented in a problem/ solution format.

Example:

"Now You Can Melt at Least 3 Inches of Fat from Your Waist in 30 Days or Less - Guaranteed!"

This headline presents the benefit of reducing fat in the waist as the #1 solution to the problem of having excess fat in the waist area.

Note: When you use a problem/solution headline, be sure you're providing a real solution or cure to a problem and not just a way to "prevent" a problem. Solutions are a hundred times easier to sell than prevention. People tend not to worry about problems until they actually exist.

Want proof? Just look at how much fast food, tobacco and alcohol today's society consumes. And look at how many people are out of shape these days. These people don't seem to be very concerned with preventing heart disease, lung cancer, obesity etc. But when they begin to experience the negative side effects, people want a solution fast.

Yes, it is unfortunate. But when you've got the solution to an overwhelming problem, you're in a powerful position to create a win/win situation. You provide the solution in exchange for money in your bank account.

3) The Flag Headline

A flag is a phrase calling for the attention of a particular person or group. Use a flag headline to attract your target audience - those most likely to buy your product or service. For example…

Attention: New Mothers!

New Exercise Safely Burns the Fat You Gained During Your Pregnancy in Less than 60 Days - Guaranteed!

You can also use the flag headline to increase response by catering your offer to readers of the publication you're advertising in. Example…

Attention: Newborn Journal Readers!

New Exercise Safely Burns the Fat You Gained During Your Pregnancy in Less than 60 Days - Guaranteed!

4) The Warning Headline

This type of headline can yield tremendous results when used properly. There are a few ways to use this approach. Your headline can propose a warning to read your message before making a purchase. Or you can use the warning to flag a specific audience. The following example uses both of these techniques.

* Warning: Dieters *

Don't eat another reduced-calorie meal until you read this startling message... Why Your Current Eating Habits May be Doing More Damage to Your Body Than Good!

5) The Testimonial Headline

This is simply a satisfied customer testimonial used as a headline. Here's an example:

"Big Boulder Protein Powder helped me pack on 11 pounds of PURE Muscle and reduce my body fat by 6.4% in only 37 days, without changing my exercise routine, and I know it can do the same for you too."

The quotes around the headline signify that it's an actual quote from a customer, giving it added validity.

When using this method, it's important that the testimonial has a strong impact. It must make a significant claim related to a major benefit of your product or service. Don't just use an "average" testimonial, or it won't have the desired effect.

A note about using numbers: Specifics beat General.

In the example above, notice that I used:

"11 pounds of muscle" instead of "over 10 pounds" and...

"reduced my body fat by 6.4%" instead of just 6% and...

"in only 37 days" instead of "less than 6 weeks".

These specific numbers make the statement more believable and will bring better results.

Another key point: Notice that I used the phrase "without changing my exercise routine". This shows the reader that the product itself (not the workout routine) was solely responsible for the results. It's crucial that your product or service is "easy" to use and gets the desired results. People buy simplicity, not complications.

Power Words for Stronger Headlines

Here are some ~~25~~ 26 Power words that will make your headline irresistible:

1. You

2. Free

3. Discover

4. Guarantee

5. New

6. Urgent

7. Perfect

8. Personalised

9. Exclusive

10. Only

11. Announcing

12. Now

13. How/How to

14. Easy

15. Health

16. Love

17. Proven

18. Save

19. Safety

20. Hurry

21. Discount

22. Deserve

23. Celebrate

24. Latest

25. Customised

26. Limited

Incorporate these words into your headline, where appropriate, and watch your response rates soar.

Headline Mistakes to Avoid at All Costs

If you want your headlines to sell (and of course you do), don't waste your time or advertising dollars on these common mistakes.

1) Don't be a comedian (even if you are one).

Don't use headlines that try to be clever, cute, or use a play on words. This is definitely NOT the way to get attention and entice readers to take action. Stick with the proven methods discussed earlier.

2) DON'T USE ALL CAPITAL LETTERS

Capitals will not make your headline more effective. People are just not accustomed to reading words in all capital letters. This just makes it more difficult on the eyes and harder to read. Occasional words may be capitalized for emphasis, but not your entire headline.

3) Don't use excessive punctuation!!!!!!!!

Besides looking amateurish, it screams "hype" from a mile away. A big turn-off.

4) Don't let graphics (or anything else) take attention away from your headline.

The headline is the most important part of your sales piece. Any distractions will hinder results. You can use graphics to enhance your sales piece, but not to distract from its purpose.

5) Don't try to get "everyone's" attention with your headline.

If you advertise with the mindset that your product or service is for everyone, you've already lost. Only a specific group of people will respond to your offer. And you should only attempt to reach that specific audience with your headline (and all your other marketing materials). This is a basic marketing principle known as "target marketing" (a great topic for a future article).

Now you have a solid foundation for crafting powerful headlines. You have 5 of the most effective headline types… power words that will make your headlines irresistible… also the most common mistakes to avoid. Use them in all your ads, sales letters, and web copy to attract more prospects and win you more sales.

USP

You need to define your unique selling point or unique selling position.

How many times have you looked at a business directory for a plumber and the ads all look the same?

Free quotes, leaking taps fixed, cheap rates. A ton of ads that all look the same.

To be successful you have to stand out from the crowd, find three things.

A better example would be..
Local Plumber on your doorstep in 90 minutes or less. I'll fix what your husband hasn't and I'll give you a 3 year 100-percent money-back guarantee.

It's sharp, to the point, funny and defective.

In the 90s when I had my radiator repair shop, I had heard about a certain insurance company forcing panel beaters to offer a lifetime guarantee on the repair work.

It's a shit deal for the panel beater.

But a very good marketing concept.

So on every new radiator I started to offer a lifetime guarantee. It wasn't long before my suppliers were complaining about what I was doing.

My advertising was 100% lifetime replacement warranty.
If our new radiator failed we would replace it absolutely free.

The suppliers would call me up and say "we will not honour your lifetime warranty" and I would reply with "and you don't have to, it has been my decision to take this on board myself."
There were some terms & conditions.
The lifetime warranty was not on the life of the vehicle but on the current owner of the car.
No I did not wish that the owner would die.

The fact is that most people don't keep the same car for longer than 5 years. the warranty on the radiator does not transfer to the new owner of the car.

The car had to come back to my shop and the coolant flushed out and changed for a service fee of $45 every 6 months.
Every coolant change service was logged, and by the time 5 Years (the average life of ownership of vehicle) was over, the customer would have spent an additional $540 with me. Since the average cost of a replacement radiator was under $300 this was a win-win situation.
Most people become apathetic they might maintain the cooling system for perhaps a year and then completely forget about it.
If they came back and did not replace the coolant, it would be the customers problem, since coolant can turn corrosive when kept in the vehicle past its use-by date.
If the customer did the right thing and followed the service procedures, and the radiator failed, I would have no problem in shouting them a free one, as they have essentially paid for it twice.

When I was selling vending machine services, our unique selling position was..

A bigger menu than any other competitor including, Thai, Chinese, Japanese and Indian dishes, In addition to your typical soft drinks and chocolate bars.

The latest payment technology.

The fact that we were a local company

During my sales presentation after creating some rapport I got down to business.

The front page of the flyer did not show a vending machine, simply because everyone has expectations with a vending machine. (The robot box in the corner full of junk food)
 I would point out on the first page, "The concept is more like a corner store in a box or a restaurant that is available 24/7 on your premises".

The next page showed all the food.

The headline

Get a healthy nutritious meal and a drink for under $9 GUARANTEED..

Even though the meals came in a box I did not have pictures of boxes of food I had photo-shopped a bunch of bowls on a nice bamboo mat with cutlery showing a high quality image of a green curry chicken, teriyaki chicken etc.
Beneath, was the pictures of all the chips and chocolate bars.

Followed by a row of drinks with beads of water like sweat on the sides, making the images very appealing.
I would say to the prospect doesn't this look absolutely amazing?
 I would flip to the back where the picture was of the vending machine and show them that it was all green power, that the machine went to sleep when not in use like a computer monitor, that it had remote monitoring and 100% backup product delivery guarantee with infrared technology in the product delivery tray.

When you sell you have to show them the product.
Whipping a half-time vending machine out of my pocket was a little difficult. I would bring over a bag loaded with chocolates and chips, healthy meals, specialty drinks.

At the end of the presentation, I would do the trial close.

"So Mary you have indicated that you were absolutely Blown Away by the menu,It's absolutely fantastic isn't it? (Tie down question).
..and it's the latest technology you can see how this vending machine will not cause customers any frustration can't you?"
"We are a local company and we are not restricted to any particular brand, So that is obviously a benefit wouldn't you agree?"
"...and you can see how this would give your staff a pay rise without it costing you a cent by them saving money on lunch without spending $15 down the local takeaway."

After you've managed to get a few YES's out of them, the deal is done. Many times I would not even have to go over the contract or price list, I would just open up the contract and say let's get some details then.

Chapter 10 - Buying Signals

Buying questions or buying signals
When people start asking questions and genuinely seeking further information on points they are concerned about, these are considered buying questions...

So you're sitting there at your meeting and out of the blue one of the prospects speaks up and says, "what colour does it come in?"

Don't mistake buying signals for raising an objection we'll talk about closing techniques in the next chapters. But a good indication is that if they are raising some points, it's because they want to know more. I mean they wouldn't still be sitting there if there was no interest at all, right?

Buying signals might not necessarily be verbal they may be communicated with body language such as leaning forward, nodding and smiling.

Questions about a delivery, warranty, payment methods, how long your company have been in business, where is your head office, are all buying signals.

The scariest one of all is the.. "how much?"
If you can solve the problem you have the sale when you notice the buying signals.
I like to leave the price to last and ask them how much they would like to pay for it?

For lot of people reading body language is intuitive.

- But a quick run-through will serve as a good reminder.

- If they are looking at their watch you have gone too long.

- If they are frowning with mouth open slightly you have surprised them.

- If they have their arms crossed they are feeling negative about what you're saying.

- If they are leaning back in the chair pressing their fingertips together they are feeling confident.

- If they are tapping their fingers or a pen, this would indicate that they are bored impatient but essentially aggravated.

Chapter 11 - Common Objections and Killer closing techniques.

Top 10 objections.

1. It's too expensive.

2. I don't like contacts.

3. I'm Already Under Contract with Someone Else.

4. I don't have time now.

5. I need to talk to my team, management or my partner.

6. I want different options, features.

7. We had one like that and it was a nightmare.

8. We only work with people we have built relationships with.

9. Just leave some info.

10. I'm not ready for this.

It's too expensive.
Avoid talking about price first up! They don't know if its too expensive or not because they don't know about the features and benefits. Many times I've given a presentation and they have not even asked about the price because things have been explained properly. The solution here is to use the Ben Franklin close discussed further on.

I don't like contacts.
Sweeten the deal, offer different, perhaps no minimum terms can be written on the front of the agreement but should never be referred to as a contract.

I'm already under contract with someone else.
Know how to help get them out of it, you might be able to raise common problems with those particular products and ask them if they have experienced problems like this. You could also offer financial compensation for the trouble of dismissing the other party. About 99% of the time no one will end up in a legal situation, suppliers want the opportunity to come back.

I don't have time now.
It really depends where this is at if your cold calling simply says, "ok, sorry" come back another time. Try to leave with details, email over some info. If you really want their business just keep going back eventually they will cave in. If they have told you that they do not have the time now after the presentation, it is likely that there is something they don't understand and could not be bothered with, and generally just want to blow you off. If they have done this at the end of your presentation thank them for letting you know that Time is Running Out. You need to trial close the next appointment open your diary and ask them, "are you happy with everything you've seen so far?" Make a date then and there to follow up.

I need to talk to my team, the manager, my partner.
This person is probably not the decision maker, always push for the decision-makers business card on the first contact. Before you make the meeting try to confirm who the person is that is authorised to sign on the dotted line. Explain to them "There are usually technical questions that arise and it's best to have those people present at the meeting."
If you let people waste your time they will. If they want to talk to the team, make arrangements to attend the tool box or lunch time meeting.

I want different options and features. This is really an opportunity to see what the customer really wants, so ask them.

"What kind of features are you looking for exactly?" then repeat the answer back, "So if it came with this feature you'll be happy to go ahead, wouldn't you? OK let's do that then."

If that feature is not available you will just have to take it up with the management, but if you can give the customer what they are looking for, you leave a memorable impression that shows your company knows how to deliver.

We had one like that and it was a nightmare.

"I'm very sorry to hear that. Can you tell me a little bit about what went wrong?"

Use the feel felt found technique discussed later. Listen emphatically.

"Please allow me the opportunity to show you how we are are not like that, our business model is completely different."

We only work with people we have built relationships with.

Sometimes this is a case of nepotism, in other words someone in the family is offering a similar service to what you do, most times they are really doing a bad job of it.

"A lot of things have changed in recent times in the way this product / service works, it's a bit like your telephone bill when you originally agreed to have that service, it was great but every now and again you need to check and make sure your still getting the optimum deal. It's at least worth your time to learn what is available in the current market, you'll be able to find out how you can get the best out of them."

I'm not ready for this.

You need to have some incentive, some bonus, Close "For any customer that moves forward with our service this month we are offering a $500 donation toward your Christmas BBQ."

Just leave some info.

"Of course you're not going to be interested now, because you are not aware of how much extra profit your company will make/ thousands of dollars in savings/ double your client base/ in a roundabout way give all your staff and visitors a pay rise without it costing you a cent, please let's trade business cards, pass me the purchase officers business card and I can email over some information."

To some, closing the deal is getting the money for the sale, to others it's getting a contract signed. Closing the deal is never comfortable, there is always that edge of your seat feeling. If you're selling a good product and your presentation has addressed all the concerns that commonly come up then the product should sell itself. Your job as a salesperson is to just point out the features & benefits, always assume that your Prospect will move forward with the purchase or service.

It's important to qualify your prospects. What I mean by that is can I afford to buy what you're selling? There's no point trying to sell your second-hand rust bucket to a guy driving a new Mercedes unless of course, you can convince him that would be a great second car for his son who just passed his driver's licence test. Everyone has accidents in their first car.

The porcupine close.

So you've noticed the buying signals and they're asking the right questions.
The porcupine close is an amusing way to make a friend of the prospect.
A lot of time the question will come up that requires a conversation killing response in regards to a yes or no.

The prospect may ask, "Does it come in dark red?"
Instead of saying 'yes' or 'no' respond with, "Would you like it in dark red?"
Prospect: " Yes, that would be fantastic"
Salesperson: "I can have it ready for you next week"

The porcupine close was named this way because what would you do if someone threw a porcupine to you for you to catch? Well, you would probably throw it right back.

Making assumptions close.

If you're starting to see some buying signals, use terminology along the lines of what colour do you prefer? What is the best day to receive the delivery, Monday or Wednesday? (this should become common practice, or even on the phone when you make an appointment). Even be so bold as to start taking notes on the contract.

The suggestive close.

No, I don't mean by being sexually provocative, but hey if that works for you.
If you're getting on well with your prospect, or if you have a good rapport from previous business dealings with them and you have the feeling that they view you as a trusted expert you can say to them,"So based on what you have explained to me, it looks like this particular item is going to be the one that works best for you, I can get it here by Friday. That works for you doesn't it?"

The urgent close.
I really love this one and watching them squirm, but make sure you're presenting to the key Decision Maker the one who signs the paperwork because if you try it on with the PA or the receptionist you're going to burn.
"So you were interested in the blue one, I know we only have a few left, and within the next 2 days will most likely be all gone, so we best get a wriggle on, please sign here."

"It will take 2 weeks to process your order and we are stopping deliveries a week before Christmas if we don't do it now, you'll have to wait till February."

The Ben Franklin Close

So the Ben Franklin Close works like this..
On a piece of paper, you draw a large 'T' or ' ✛ '

The Ben Franklin Close

	Current provider or comp	YOUR OFFER
Cheap can drinks		Cans, Bottles
Chips /Choc		Chips/ chocolates
		Gluten free
		Natural Chips
		All major Brands
		Organic options
		Credit card payments
		Smart device pay
		Talking Machine
		Latest tech
		Local
		Aesthetically pleasing
		Vegan alternatives
		Hi-Protein items
		Thai, Chinese, Indian Meals

In this example, I've used Vending Machines over service.
On the left side you put the current provider, or if they don't have a provider but instead have a proposal to provide the service.
On the right-hand side on the top you write your company name.

..and say along the lines of "So here we have your current provider, he's got some cheap canned drinks in an old vending machine, and that's a little unfair because he has some chips and chocolates as well".

"Here on the right side is the difference in service that we are offering. We have CANS of drinks but we also have bottles, we have triple the range of chips and 4 times the amount of chocolate selections, as you can see from the product list that I gave you it's 3 pages long. from looking at this vending machine there are 30 selections but many of them have been doubled up, essentially leaving you with only several different but similar items.

We have items for every cultural requirement and dietary need. We have gluten-free and chemical free options, there are items and chips available for someone who wants a plant-based diet. We also offer healthy juices, energy drinks, milk drinks, sports drinks and in addition to that we use the latest technology, it's virtually impossible for you not to get your product because we're already using next year's model. We are local and we support the firefighters we actually gave them a free vending machine, we support two different charitable organisations and every Christmas we will give you a free Christmas hamper! All of that in a very specialised vending machine they can also deliver healthy meals and receive payments with everything from Cash to the latest smart device payment method."

So that's what you do to minimise your opposition's offer, keep going with all the benefits and features of what **your** offer is.

" As you can see I'm offering you the latest Mercedes Kompressor, with heated seats satellite navigation as opposed to wanting to accept a rusty 1955 Volkswagen, with a broken AM radio."

"So now you can understand why the cost of our can drinks are only a few cents more. You can really see the value here can't you?" (trial close).

Prospect agrees.

When I am near the end of the presentation I summarise what was discussed.

"So now, Mr Smith, I know you're completely blown away by the extensive menu that we offer, yes?"

Prospect agrees.

" ..and you can see now with the latest technology how there's very little chance of a breakdown, and that has to be a major benefit, RIGHT?"

Prospect agrees.

"..you have got to be happy when I have explained to you, when you're dealing with us you're dealing with a local company that is family-run. Someone is available at all times and is not some call centre?"

Prospect agrees.

"That's fantastic let's get some details now. Perfect, just sign on the dotted line."

It's a good idea to have your paperwork out from the beginning, it shows that you will not tolerate tyre kickers.

Many books on sales mentioned this sometimes awkward situation, many of the same books will tell you to ask for permission. I think that's utter bullshit. The Client needs to be aware that you're not there to blow smoke up their arse. Simply explain to them that you are going to be taking some notes so that nothing is forgotten. You don't want to waste their valuable time or cost them by mistake on your behalf.

Sometimes you'll get a prospect that doesn't show much interest or just listens, or it is hard for you to determine which direction things are heading.

Just simply ask, "So how do you feel so far about the things we have discussed?"

Sometimes you can notice your prospect drifting off, you can give the same presentation 100 times and most people are fairly proactive if you're interesting enough. On the odd occasion, the part of the presentation you're discussing is not what is of most interest to them. You might be talking about the technology when they really want to know what colour it comes in, you may have to adjust how much depth to go into when discussing a particular aspect. A way to handle it is to simply just pause, that tends to bring them back fairly quickly.

Chapter 12 - Follow-up

If you can't get the deal done in one meeting make sure you open your diary and offer your prospect 1 or in a pinch 2 options of time slots of when you'll be able to reconvene with them.

If you find difficulty getting people on the phone try ringing early in the morning, usually about 15 minutes before the estimated start time. Mondays and Fridays usually don't work so good, people are fairly negative on Monday and Friday, they just want to get out of there. Use that time to create your reports or if you're involved in digital marketing spend that time with the AdWords account or social media.
With the vending project that I do at the moment, I make it my mission to close the deal on the first meeting. For me, it takes sometimes 3, for others it can take up to 5. (and that can be 5 attempts to get a meeting, and another 5 to close the deal).

Chapter 13 - Mind-power

Everything first manifests itself in the mind. The mind is a very powerful thing. Imagine yourself in a big house with a big car and a big bank account. This is how rich people think. The first thing that must come to the mind is desire, then the imagination. Without imagination there is nothing. Think of the great films of our time. Star Wars, Harry Potter, Titanic, The Marvel movies adapted from comics etc. Think of the fantastic special effects wizardry, the awesome visual aspects of the film set. These things started first in someone's mind. This just goes to show that anything is possible once it is imagined. So far you have learned the tools to be a great salesperson, you have learned that you must set goals. You know that these goals must be specific, you must be able to visualise yourself achieving these goals. Whether the goal be the number of sales for the week or an amount of money at the end of the week, or as much as seeing into the future to envision yourself with the big house and the big car 10 years down the track. Now you will learn to program your mind to achieve your conscious desires.

Remember learning to drive? Do you remember having to recall the procedure to start the car? Insert key, put a seat belt on, make sure the gear is in neutral or park, put your foot on the brake, turn the key, check mirrors, signal, apply light pressure to the accelerator, move slowly forward, look over your shoulder etc. Now you just jump into the car and drive. Sometimes you remember getting into the car and arriving at your destination without remembering how you got there. This is because your subconscious has learned the pattern. Just like eating and speaking you don't struggle with these tasks, they are patterns that are ingrained into your subconscious mind.

How does this work? Up until we are about three years of age, our brains are operating in alpha mode.

So what is alpha mode? Alpha is what is known as the primary brain pattern between 7-16 Hz or seven to sixteen cycles per second. When our brains operate in this spectrum, information is loaded directly to the subconscious, therefore creating an automatic pattern. Just like a photographic memory.

Wow! How can I get some alpha? Everybody goes into alpha at least two times a day. As you awaken, between awake and asleep you enter the alpha zone. You know that half-awakened drowsy feeling? This is also the stage between when you doze off to sleep, just before you begin to dream. This is the most powerful learning stage that is easily attainable. Ultimate stage, however, is that of Theta.

Alpha 7-16 Hz.

Beta 16-25 Hz.

Delta 0.5-3 Hz.

Theta 4-7 Hz.

Your brain is like a cars gearbox, IT NEEDS to use all of these states of mind. If you drive your car without changing through all of the gears, your car is likely to break down. Just like if you don't get enough sleep or enough time to reflect then you usually become stressed out. Let me explain. As you read this book your brain will shift from beta to alpha. As you relax and drift in and out of what you are reading your brain will shift. When your imagination kicks in, this is when alpha waves are most active. Now imagine that you are just drifting off to sleep, you are also in alpha. Now you begin to dream. You start to dream about walking and you trip, your body jumps and you almost wake up. But you just drift off again. Now you are in Theta. You spend a little of your sleep stage here but just travel into Delta. Delta is the deepest state of sleep. And when you begin to awaken your brain will drift into Theta then Alpha and finally Beta.

Beta is like the fourth gear. This is where your brain is mostly. This is also when the left side of the brain is most active. The left side of the brain is the most dominant. The left side of the brain is responsible for the analytical function like mathematics, reading etc. The right side of the brain is the creative side, it is responsible for your imagination intuition, artistic, musical, spatial and inspirational thinking. It is also where your subconscious lies.

Mind Power and Magic

Let us just take a moment to think about what people have achieved. Not only the great scientists of our time. But everything that has happened in this last century just passed, and especially technology in the last 30 years. Not only the invention of the computer but the refining of technology. One of the first computers built by International Business Machines IBM was the size of a small kitchen and could only do basic math, 25 years later I write this book with a laptop computer and voice recognition software. I can play games on the laptop, work with advanced mathematical spreadsheets, track my family tree, and surf the internet. After that, I can upload the files to a palm-size computer (Tablet or Smartphone) and work on these whilst traveling. When IBM had developed the computer, a journalist asked the CEO about the international market for computers. The response was "Perhaps three to four internationally." Apart from all the technology, just think for a moment about sheer mind power. Like breaking the one-minute barrier for running the mile or think of meditating Zen monks that sit naked in the mountains whilst snow falls around them, freezing the plants and water. I once saw a man on a television show put 100 stainless steel hooks through his skin and hang from a metal frame. A martial arts master can throw a punch that stops one inch from impact and cause a bruise on the other side of the target site. Just like a bullet exit wound.

In some religions, members believe if hate is focused enough on an individual, something bad will befall them, or they may even die.

Warts are told to go away, and people can walk on hot coals pain free. Breathing and blood pressure can be slowed to the point of artificially inducing a coma-like state.

Robert Louis Stevenson in one of his books *Across the plains* devotes a whole chapter to dreams. He was a vivid dreamer and had the persistent habit of giving specific instructions to his subconscious every night prior to sleep. He would request his subconscious would evolve stories for him whilst he slept. For example, if his funds were getting low his demand to his subconscious was 'give me a good thrilling novel which will be marketable and profitable'. His subconscious responds magnificently.

Stevenson says, "these little brownies (the intelligent powers of the subconscious mind) can tell me a story piece by piece, like a serial, and keep me, it's supposed creator, all the while in total ignorance of where they aim." He added, "the parts of my work which is done when I am up and about is by no means mine since it goes to show that the brownies have a hand in it even then."

So what is this phenomena? All of these things can be achieved in Alpha and Theta states. Day dreaming, meditation, religion, mesmerizing, Alpha therapy, faith healing, psychic power, hypnosis, prayer and there are many other names for it however it is all the same thing.

In order to get there you have to consciously recognize this state of mind, so that you can more easily get into this state and deepen it so as to achieve better results.

It is best to practice these techniques in order to start working with the candle technique.

The candle technique.

Dim the lights, and light a candle. Sit in a comfortable chair. Place the candle at eye level, on a coffee table or candle stand or stack of books, or all of these, however, make sure that whatever you do is safe. We don't want a fire or anything. Now get comfortable and stare at the candle flame, do not remove your thoughts and attention from the centre of the flame not even for a single moment, just concentrate and relax. Let your mind relax, let your body relax. Do this for about 20 minutes. This is a great stress reliever. It is a known fact that if you don't use all the gears in your CARS GEARBOX then it will break down. Just as if you don't use all of the brain waves you will break down. The term "Burn Out or Burnt Out" is used for stressed-out people who overwork or have overworked themselves. Overwork results in overuse of Beta wave patterns and a lack of Alpha wave. I know this, as I have been there.

When you have finished, speak your desire and blow out the candle. Just like a birthday cake making a wish. Many people will now be upset to know that the act of blowing out candles and making a wish, actually goes back to pagan times and folk magic, as in witchcraft. if you're uncomfortable with this just do the relaxation part.

Relaxation technique

You may want to record this scripting onto a device of your choosing. Sit or lie on a comfortable sofa. Close your eyes. Concentrate and relax. Say to yourself relax. Play the recording or if you have memorised the script say in your minds voice...

" My big toe is relaxing, my other big toe is relaxing, I can feel a warm tingling relaxation feeling penetrating into my big toes. This relaxation feeling is spreading across the rest of my toes. This relaxation feeling is traveling further across the soles of my feet and the warm tingling feeling is penetrating into every nerve and fibre of my feet. This relaxation feeling now travels further into my ankles. My feet and ankles are now totally relaxed. Now the warm tingly relaxation feeling is traveling into my calf muscles and further around my shins and up into my knee caps. As my legs feel heavy my thighs and hamstrings are relaxing. Now both my feet and legs feel heavy and totally relaxed. This relaxation travels into my hips and pelvis, and moves into the spine, soothing, relaxing and completely calming. The warm tingling relaxation feeling travels further up my spine and into my shoulders, a nice calming sensation. Now my upper body is also relaxed and feels heavy. My shoulders and biceps and triceps are relaxing and feeling heavy. Now traveling down to my forearms and wrists and is now moving into my hands and fingers. My arms are now totally relaxed, warm and tingly from shoulder to fingertip. The warm relaxation feeling is now moving up to my neck and relaxing all the neck muscles. It is now traveling into the back of my skull and over the top of my head and into the muscles of my face, my jaw relaxes and drops slightly. My whole body is now totally relaxed, the warm tingly relaxation feeling is penetrating every muscles, nerve, and fibre. Every bone is totally relaxed. "

Now say to yourself "I am a fantastic salesperson, I can sell anything. I can sell ice to Eskimos, oil to Texans, and sand to the Arabs. I am a money magnet. Money comes easily to me. I always sell over my head. I am friendly and easy-going, but always in control."

(At this point if you are in bed you may wish to just stay asleep. The above suggestions can be modified to anything positive-for example "I am a great lover" or if you want to give up a habit like smoking "I am able to breathe easy, I enjoy the fresh air, I am a non smoker" never say I feel sick when I smoke or I don't smoke. This is because the subconscious can't understand the word don't, do not, can't or won't. The subconscious interprets "I don't smoke" as "I smoke". Using negative suggestions may work for a short time, but won't have any lasting results..

Tip-you may want to add that when you touch your thumb and forefinger together that you will go into a deeper state of sleep than you are now*)*.

In a moment I am going to wake up. On the count of three, I will be fully awake and feeling fantastic.

1. Heart rate is increasing, muscle tone returning.

2. Feeling more awake now, coming to the surface.

3. Wide awake now, eyes open, fully awake now.

Take a deep breath.

Tip-as you say the first half of the script, use a slow-flowing relaxing tone. When you start to wake yourself, use a faster urgent tone.

Use the candle and relaxation techniques for three to four weeks, everyday or every second day. This will help you become used to the feeling of being in the Alpha state.

Now you can use the speed techniques.

Alpha technique

Close your eyes and imagine a cinema screen, and the film is about to start. You see the number 3 flashed on the screen, the number is characteristic of the type with a revolving dial. The number 3 is shown 3 times then the number two is shown 3 times, then the number one 3 times.

Now mentally count backwards from 30 to 0 and as you do so feel yourself relaxing deeper, and deeper. When you reach 0 you will have reached the Alpha zone.

Visualize now a lake on a moonlit night. You see the light on the ripples. Now use mental visualization to flatten the ripples.

Now say to yourself "I am a fantastic salesperson, I can sell anything. I can sell ice to Eskimos, oil to Texans, and sand to the Arabs. I am a money magnet. Money comes easily to me. I always sell over my head. I am friendly and easy-going, but always in control"

In a moment I am going to wake up. On the count of three, I will be fully awake and feeling fantastic.

1.heart rate is increasing, muscle tone returning.

2. Feeling more awake now, coming to the surface.

3. Wide awake now, eyes open, fully awake now.

How to make a million dollars

1. Set your goal in stone.

Write down your goal (I want one million dollars or a beach house etc.). Then dedicate yourself to its attainment with unswerving zeal. Like a mad man.

2. Develop a plan with a deadline.

Plan your progress hour by hour, day by day, month by month. Write down the date that you will achieve your goal on the same sheet of paper.

3. Create a sincere desire for the things you want in life.

Visualise the things you want, feel it in your heart. Desire is the greatest motivator, it makes success a habit.

4. Trust your intuition and your ability.

Defeat does not exist. Do not entertain the possibility of defeat. Focus on your strengths and forget about weakness.

5. Create an unstoppable determination to follow through with your plan, regardless of obstacles, criticism, circumstances or what others say, think, or do.

There is no such thing as luck. Go and create the situation you want to be in to get and take what you deserve.

(My first company turned, I have generated a million dollars plus for sales clients, holding onto it is a different story).

My goal is to:

I will achieve this by:

This goal will be accomplished on:

Photocopy the above plan and fill in the blanks be as graphic as you can. Paste or tape the photocopy where you will see it every day. And read your goals every day. In the morning, say to yourself, what am I doing today to get me closer to my goal?

Sometimes it is best to not tell friends and relatives about your goals. For example, you may desire to start your own sales and marketing company. One that contracts to other businesses to attract more customers for them. You may desire to become a marketing consultant and charge one hundred dollars an hour. You may want to do something out of the ordinary.

When I would have a new business idea, my father would always tell me that it would never work. My friends would sometimes say "you need to do this or that before you can do that!"

Now when they ask me what I'm doing next, I tell them you will see when it happens.

This is the best way to ward off all the 'experts'. It seems really funny how people with no experience whatsoever suddenly become experts in **your** chosen field of endeavour.

X equals an unknown factor, a spurt is a drip under pressure. (Expert.)

Recite your goals like a mantra 6 times before you go to bed. It usually takes 6-7 times before something is remembered, from pop songs to phone numbers.

When using self-hypnosis tell your sub-conscious that you have a photographic memory and that you can recall things on demand. You will be surprised how well this can work.

OH, a note, when using self-hypnosis, stick to one thing for at least a month. Don't say to yourself "I'm a non-smoking, fat burning, great salesman.", as this is not focused.

It's best to work on one thing at a time.

Selling your home

Why do some homes listed for sale sit on the market unsold for many months whereas others sell quickly in a few days or weeks? The physical condition of your home, your skill or that of the real estate agent to properly market your home to as many qualified buyers as possible. The number of buyers in the local marketplace and desirability of your home compared to other nearby homes now available for sale, are factors as well. Realtors will tell you that if a home doesn't sell within 90 days it is probably overpriced. However, too high an asking price is not always the reason a home doesn't sell. It's how you write the ad and show them the house.

Whether you get top dollar for your home will depend on many factors, such as local economic conditions, supply of homes for sale and the property market.

Mistakes

Most home builders are very good at giving buyers what they want -- a "red-ribbon deal." That's a home in near-perfect "display home" move-in condition where all the buyer must do is turn the key in the front door and move in. Buyers are willing to pay top dollar for these homes.

But what are most home sellers offering? Fixer-uppers! Or at least homes with problems. As I browse through our local Multiple Listings I see buyer-discouraging phrases in the listing: "Seller will credit $10,000 for roof repairs".

"Seller prefers 'as is' sale," "Needs 24-hour notice to show," "Now vacant, tenants are finally out," "renovators dream," I could go on, but I'm sure you get the idea why these homes won't sell easily and certainly not for the highest price possible. Sellers and agents should present the home in its best possible light. Avoid negatives. If a house needs fixing up, do the work before putting it on the market. That house needing $30,000 of work must be in pretty bad shape. Very few home buyers are willing, or capable, of both buying a home and tackling major repair work. Yes, there are buyers for fixer-upper homes, but they will usually buy only at greatly discounted prices, far below the house's market value if it were in good condition.

Look at your home through a buyer's eyes

Pretend you are buying your home. Walk around each room and the exterior and jot down the good and bad aspects you would spot if you were buying your home. Look especially for the need to paint, clean and repair. Throw out unneeded items. The goal should be to get your home into "display home" condition if you want to get its best price possible.

For example, as I look at the living room of my home if I were selling I would write down that it needs fresh paint, fireplace cleaning, new carpets, and furniture rearrangement to make the room look larger. The cost? Less than $1,000 to present a neat, welcoming look for buyers, improve my home saleability, and even increase its market value.

Most homes just need a "freshening up" to make them marketable for top dollar. New paint is the most profitable improvement you can make, so give serious thought to painting the interior and exterior.

Inspections

I am constantly amazed at home sellers who do not have a professional inspection of their home before listing it for sale. Then they are surprised when the *buyer's* inspector finds unexpected defects, thus allowing the buyer to negotiate the sales price downward (often far more than repairs would cost). The cost of a professional inspection is only $200 to $300 -- that's petty cash compared to the sales price of your home.

Have any serious problems, such as dangerous wiring, promptly corrected. If it's not critical, such as minor gutter rust that isn't leaking, skip it but disclose the report to the buyer.

In addition to a professional inspection, have any customary inspections used in your area completed before the sale. In my area, for example, it's customary to obtain a termite or pest control inspection report.

Agents

Once your home is in excellent condition, interview at least three successful realty agents about listing it for sale. *Do this even if you plan on selling your home by yourself.* Each agent should give you a Comparative Market Analysis (CMA) that will show recent sales prices of nearby comparable homes, asking prices for homes in the area, and the agent's opinion of your home's fair market value.

As you will see from these CMAs, your home doesn't have an exact market value. Instead, it has a range of values based on the expert opinions of the real estate agents.

Once you've interviewed your three agents, select one who makes things happen. Let me give you an example: Last Saturday, I phoned a local real estate to inquire about a house and left a message on his answering machine. He didn't call me back until Monday afternoon. Is that the kind of real estate agent you want to work with you? I hope not.

You've done everything correctly. You got your home into that 'first-class condition' before interviewing at least three successful local real estate agents about listing it for sale. After asking lots of questions and reviewing their CMAs and client references, you selected the best agent for a 90-day exclusive listing with an asking price at your home's fair market value. Fortunately, you can offer seller financing by carrying back a second mortgage to lower the buyer's cash down payment. The local market for home sales is good, especially at this time of year. Your house should sell within the customary 90 days because your agent is aggressive, hardworking and successful.

A few weeks after your home hits the market, your agent phones to report another agent has a purchase offer. When it is presented to you, it's disappointing because it's about 5 per cent below your asking price. Since you've listed your home at a realistic price, just slightly above its market value as shown by the CMAs you received from the three agents interviewed, you're insulted by the low offer. You want to counteroffer at the full asking price. Instead, your agent counsels you not to get greedy if you really want to sell. So you make a more reasonable counter offer below your asking price. After some haggling back and forth, you and the buyer agree on a price. The two agents handle all the inspections, the financing and the eventual closing at the highest possible price. Congratulations!

Chapter 14 - Sell your car

Here's how to sell your car on the Internet and get more than what you paid for it when you bought it second hand.

I do this all the time.
Initially, if you buy a car you should really check it out and know what you're talking about. Find as many problems with it as possible.

Another trick to get the price down is to say to them, "Your car is fantastic and it's absolutely worth every cent you're asking for it and I would really love this car but the problem is I'm $200 short of what you're asking."
It's best if you pull out a wad of cash, counted out to them and say, "Come on, let's go, what do you say?"
It's even better if you're still holding the keys.
"Seriously I would love this car I will look after it, I will wash it every weekend, I know you need to get it off your front lawn so let's do this now and then you can get on with doing what you want to do instead of having to put up with tyre kickers for the rest of the day."

Most people write their ads like a **car for sale**, automatic transmission, 100,000km, good tyres.
So here's how to get more for it, and fast, particularly works well with women.

Hello, my name is Oscar, I'm a green Hyundai Excel, I used to be very happy when my mum would take me on drives down to the beach oh she would play her favourite music 50 watt sound system. I would get a bath and a wax every Sunday and she loves me very much. But now I'm very sad I sit here on the front lawn. Daddy bought mummy a new car, so now I just sit here alone. No music is played anymore, just silence. I don't understand what I have done wrong, I am a good little car, I've always been well maintained and I don't have that many kilometres. I overheard daddy saying that he was going to take me to the wrecking yard, where strange people would pull parts off my body, I feel very lonely and scared, will you please come and rescue me? I promise to be a good car.

I know it's quite evil, but did you feel like you were almost brought to tears?

Emotional selling is a very, very powerful concept.
Every time I sold a car like this I've got at least $500 more, than what I actually paid for it.

People just want to rescue the car.
Obviously in your advertising, you would go into as much detail as possible about all the features and benefits.
Also detail the car so that it is immaculate including the engine bay, by using degrease, and pressure wash it entirely.
Get a $10 can of black enamel and touch up anything missing some paint. After the paint dries, spray the engine with tyre gloss silicone spray. Make sure the car smells nice inside. clean the wheels entirely and put Tyre Shine on them, clean all the windows, vacuum the carpet and the boot. Use a high gloss wax on the paintwork. Use metal polish on any Chrome badge work. Pick up some external mats.
..and don't forget to use the sales techniques that you have learnt in this book to get top dollar for your second-hand vehicle.

Here's a great little mind trick to get people to agree with you.

The Scientifically-Proven Method For Getting People To Say "Yes" :

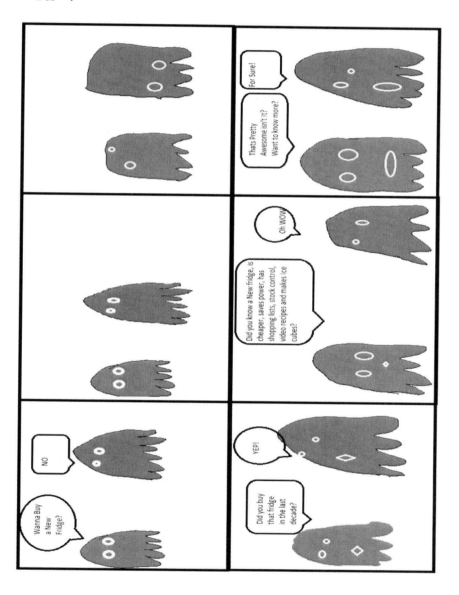

And you can continue from there - the person is hooked.

The trick is to start with something you know they'll say yes to.

Then you can follow up with something that's difficult to say no to. Then you can either ask about their preferences or ask clarifying questions to solidify a yes.

Finally, ask the thing you really wanted to ask, and you'll most likely get a Yes to that as well.

Here's an example from dating:

"Are you spontaneous?" Yes

"Are you an adventurous person?" Sure

"Have you ever done anything that was a little crazy?" Yeah!

"Have you ever made out with someone you just met?" I think so!

"Wouldn't you regret it if you didn't?" Probably...

"Do you have some free time during the week?" Yeah

"Wanna go grab a drink?" Sure!

... you got yourself a date :)

For those interested in how it works - here's the science behind this mind trick:

The brain has an emotional feedback loop that causes you to seek out sensation and stimulation that will keep you feeling however you're feeling right now, either good or bad, and avoid anything that will make you feel different. That even applies to say "yes" and "no."

There is a study called "Better think before agreeing twice - Mere agreement: A similarity-based persuasion mechanism," published in the International Journal of Research in Marketing in 2010, which states:

> "The present paper shows that the frequency of people's compliance with a request can be substantially increased if the requester first gets them to agree with a series of statements unrelated to the request but selected to induce agreement. We label this effect the 'mere-agreement effect' and present a two-step similarity-based mechanism to explain it.
>
> Across five studies, we show that induced mere agreement subtly causes respondents to view the presenter of the statements as similar to themselves, which in turn increases the frequency compliance with a request from that same person. We support the similarity explanation by showing that the effect of the agreement on compliance is suppressed when an agreement is induced to indicate dissimilarity with the interviewer, when the request is made by some other person, and when the artificially high level of agreement is made salient. We also validate the practical relevance of the mere-agreement persuasion technique in a field study. We discuss how the mere-agreement effect can be broadly used as a tool to increase cooperation and be readily implemented in marketing interactions."

Pretty amazing, right?

The fact that you've gotten someone to agree with you on several statements in a row makes them significantly more likely to agree with your next statement, even if it's entirely unrelated to those previous ones. Getting people to comply is a very interesting experiment.

This is a second-hand story.

A circus that had been around for some time would travel into town and in the hopes of promoting the event, it would Park it's highly painted and sign written trucks on various highly visible street corners, several representatives of the circus would door knock in the hope of asking the occupant of the house if it would be OK if they could put our very large banner on the front fence. Most people would refuse. however, if they offered some free tickets, occasionally someone would agree to have the large banner on the front fence.

The best practice, however, was to simply ask if they could put a small card on the fence. The circus found that they could get a strike rate of around 90%.

If they would then go back to the house in a few days and say to the occupants that a lot of people mentioned that they could not see the sign because it was too small and if it would be ok to put a bigger one on, people would again comply. If they went back a third time and offered free tickets they found that most people would comply with having the largest banner on the front fence.

The police have been known to use variations of this technique. The good cop, bad cop routine is one that is portrayed in Hollywood movies.

The good cop approaches the suspect and says things along the lines of how the crime that they are suspected of committing isn't such a big deal if they could just help out with some information. the bad cop comes in screaming and yelling and telling the suspect about all the bad things that are going to happen in jail and how the suspects life will be destroyed. The bad cop gets aggressive shoves the suspect around, pushes around the furniture in the interview room storming out, in an attempt to rattle the suspect. The good cop shows up again tries to act like a friend, saying things to the suspect along the lines of... "you can tell me what happened it's all OK, I'm here to help you and do my best for you".

It is a very extreme example of the whole sales process.

Using disturbance, followed by influence, then some more disturbance.

Chapter 15 - The elevator pitch.

So what's an elevator pitch, and why do you want one.

Sometimes your Prospect is very difficult to get hold of, and the name was coined in how to sell to someone if you had approximately half a minute in an elevator.

If you search on the Internet you'll be loaded with really bad examples that tell you to basically ..

- Introduce yourself

- Summarise what you do

- Explain what you want

- Finished with a call to action

- Be confident

For me, saying something like, " Hi, my name is Guy and I have awesome vending machines", is a really shitty approach.

How about try, "Wow, the range in your vending machine is pretty limited I really felt like a juice, do your staff get much use out of it?"

This is a good Icebreaker.
You can then move on, talk about the best points of the product.
Your call-to-action is to get some Face-time with the prospect.

Chapter 16 - The Negative Approach

Many people are going to raise their eyebrows at this one. Sometimes a negative approach will finalise the sale.

When you've been doing sales for sometime you develop an instinct that it is all just a power play. One way to handle this is if you get the feeling they really want your product but then start making excuses as to why they should move forward, you simply take the product away from them. What I mean by that is if they start hammering you with really stupid objections. You will get a feel for it after some experience in dealing with your particular product or service.

So I went to see a small carpentry factory in regards to a vending service, at the meeting there were dogs running around in the office and they barely qualified with the number of people there but I knew that it would be OK because of the hard work aspect. There were many interruptions during the meeting with people just walking in and butting in. It was hard to paint a picture due to the lack of attention by the staff members at the meeting. I got the job over the line and the contract signed. Normally my client wants a two-year contract, but they wanted no responsibility and for the pure fact that they weren't listening to most of the presentation, so it was hard to build confidence in talking about some of the fortune 500 companies that utilise my client Vending service.

so later I was hit with the below email ..

Hi Guy,

Thank you for coming out yesterday and meeting the team.

Just wanted to confirm a few things from our meeting yesterday.

- (Client Company) is not locked into a contract with (Vending service) with using the vending machine on-site, however as noted on the form signed yesterday the vending machine must stay on-site for a minimum of 2 weeks.

- (Client company) is not responsible for any damage to the vending machine whilst in use at (Client company) factory.

- As per conversation yesterday it was a concern by the team that the dust may affect the vending machine but as advised by yourself the machine is not affected by the dust.

- There is no cost for the machine or stock that is filled. Visits to restock the machine is no cost to (Client company)

- Location on site approved by Guy

We have marked the selected items we would like to stock the machine with which is attached. Are you able to advise your minimum price for the item and we can decide on the price to help meet the target minimum of $100 a week.

We would like to have the machine by the 1st of December if we are able too. Are you able to let us know the date the machine will be delivered so we are able to ensure the area is clean and ready.

Kind Regards,

(Client name)

Designer

My response..

Hi (Client Name),

I hope you are well, and B Shared those goodies :)

Thank you for asking, and I am delighted to clear things up,

I have CC'd my boss Mr M

Its hard when there is a lot going on in an office, and a bit of info to be absorbed.

Everything you have pointed out is essentially correct. So Covering our discussions. **No minimum terms** = the rules apply to work place Health and Safety, Insurance and ownership, however **no locked in time.** So you can cancel anytime for any reason, our service is a partnership, and about building relationships. If something is wrong we ask that you allow us the opportunity to address it. If the matter can't be resolved then *please give us a couple of weeks* to let the stock run down and book the sensitive freight company to collect it.

Damage- Do you plan on hitting it? If this is a major concern, its a red flag for me, and perhaps we should not proceed, If I loan you my car would you bring it back with a full tank and washed? Just take care of it. If someone has a problem with it call us, (the service number is on the front) don't kick it. We have never claimed damages on any customer in 30+ years of business. Sometimes accidents happen and we know that, but if you have a worker there that behaves violently get rid of them.

- **DUST**- I believe we have picked the best location. The machine has air filters, Perhaps whoever sweeps the floor might use the airline to blow it off every now and again. Wood dust is better than metal dust, its upfront and as close as it can be to fresh air. (We have the same types in Coal Mines and Metalworks, Not my first Rodeo).

- **No Cost** - That's Correct, we loan you the Machine and service it for free. The only time you part with Money is when you purchase out of it. So shout your buddies and let the workers next door know they can use it and also every truck that pulls up. :)

- **Approval** - Final approval is by Mr M. It's my job to assess if it will work for both parties. Good for you, good for us, everyone smiles.

Some really yummy picks on that list (it's like a Genie and the 3wishes isn't it?) I'll forward to Mr M (aka Willy Wonka) don't worry about pricing.
Mr M will work out the best price to hit your targets. If we base that on a single $2 coin for a can of drink, we can base the other items around that. **We have to keep things cheap** to encourage usage.
ie you went to the lunch shop because you felt like a Burger (or chicken salad), the lunch shop lady will say "Would you like can of drink?"

But you know your Vending machine is a lot cheaper and colder.

It feels great to clear things up, don't you agree?
I'm happy that you have reached out with these items.
I've been busy getting things moving for you.
Have a Great Weekend (Client name)!
Mr M will buzz you next week and set delivery times with you.

Sounds Great, Yeah?

Kindest Regards Guy

You can see by the above response it was a polite SmackDown,

I know my client would not be too phased if the deal didn't go through.
you're not going to win them all but sometimes a great tactic is to serve it
back.
There was another time when I probably got up and walked out on a
different and difficult client.

They had filled out our contact form on the Internet. If someone doesn't
call you straight away however, instead chooses to fill out a contact form
it's a good chance that they are just looking for more information.
I called them up and ask them if all the decision-makers could be present
at the meeting and they agreed. I then confirm that at the meeting, but
when it came to the crunch the decision maker was not actually there. I
used the presumptive close. They were having problems with the current
vending provider, saying that he was not filling the machines up enough
and his prices were too high. In my mind, his prices were quite
reasonable, and from the way the meeting was going they were a bunch
of demanding little bitches.

The meeting was frustration after frustration, and demand after demand.

I promised to give them a better deal with the price and asked if I could
get a signature when they explained that they were happy to move
forward.

When it came to the crunch, the decision-maker had responded to the 'go-between' that later in the day, she would have to have a look at everything and come back to me before signing off.

The 'go-between' indicated that everything was going to move forward so I asked them if they could get the paperwork signed and then email it back to me, however, since I am here, I would measure the doors. One of the other girls came in and told me that I was not allowed to measure the doors.

That was it, I told them "thanks for wasting my time, I really feel sorry for the current operator, and understand the reasons that he is not looking after you. You are simply a pain in the arse. I don't want to do business with you, don't contact me again. I grabbed my things and promptly left."

Chapter 17 - Other Closes

"Sell me this pen", hails fourth Leonardo DiCaprio in the movie that every salesperson should watch, the *Blockbuster film,* **The Wolf of Wall Street.**

Former stockbroker Jordan Belfort was an absolute genius at manipulating people to buy.

Somewhere between now and the time the film was in the cinemas, recruitment agencies have thought this was a fun idea to throw into a job interview, but it is a very powerful experiment.

Just throw the candidate a pen and see if they can sell it to you.

It's not a new trick, one of the most famous marketing men the century would be Zig Ziglar. Zig was interviewed by Johnny Carson, "They say the world's greatest salesman, so sell me this ashtray."

The pitch went something like this..

Zig says to Johnny
"Before I can sell it to you, I need to know why you would want it ?".
Johnny said something along the lines of, "Well it's a nice looking ashtray and it looks well made."
Zig: "that's great but you have to tell me what it's worth to you"
Johnny "$20".

Zig: "Sold"

What can we learn from this? It works if someone's in a showroom looking at a car, or in a retail environment.
It also gets information from the customer by letting them tell you what it's worth. I have done this quite a bit, going into the details of the features and benefits of the product. A lot of times the customer will offer more than you are actually expecting.

In the film, Jordan asks his colleague, to sell him the pen.
"Can you sign your name on that napkin ?"
Jordan. "I don't have a pen."

In the film, this is made to be about supply and demand.
Other sales gurus will tell you, do not start waffling on about features and benefits, instead asked questions like "How long have you been looking to buy a pen?"

Again, it's a good tip if someone is actually looking for your product but what if they're not? What if it is your job to sell something, that, up until the point you contacted them, they had no idea that they even needed or cared about your product?

The very first step to a cold sale is to **identify a problem.**

I don't know if it's true or not, but there was a story going around, that NASA spent millions of dollars developing a pen that could write in zero gravity. The Russians decided to use a pencil.
Here is an example of a hard Sell...

Sell me this pen

1. Salesperson hands over a small eraser. Prospect asks "what's this for?"
   "You can have that for free".
   "What does it do?"
   "It's a Magic Eraser that erases a special pen ink, and the coolest thing is, it only works with a special pen."
   "This, very nice looking pen that is worthy of any high-level executive, encased in fine silver, and writes on just about any surface when similar pens sell for $100 its only $20, and if you can pay me now I'll give you 2".

2. "But I'm not looking for a pen."
"So tell me, have you often picked up a pen to find that the ink has dried up?"
"Yes, that happens occasionally."
"Have you ever had a pen smudge?"
"Yes."
"Can you tell me about the last time you used a pen and what you did with it?"

"Well, I was taking notes at a meeting."
"What else do you do with a pen?"
"I signed important documents."
"It feels good when you've made an important decision to sign off on something, doesn't it?"
"Yes."
"So this very attractive pen, clad in sterling silver, with smudge-proof ink, and a nice smooth ballpoint would be a very good purchase to sign off on important documentation. Take it and feel the weight, see how it's perfectly balanced? For an important person like yourself you should not be seen with just any old pen, wouldn't you agree?"
"Yes."
"This is a prestige pen, and they normally sell for $50, I know you can think of someone who would like this pen as a gift? For you today, I'm happy to part with it for $40, and I know you're going to now think of someone else who would absolutely love this prestige pen as a gift. So I'm happy to provide an extra one, For only another $30. So that's 2 pens, normally worth $100 you can take now for just $70, But that's only if we do this today, isn't that just a steal?"

If you've looked up how to sell this pen on-line, you've probably come across this question being asked at job interviews and a lot of responses on the blogs that you've come across are very simple. The reason people blog is to make money from advertising. But if you do come across this question at a job interview, try not to use the response from blogs you come across because 5 other candidates probably have used the same answer.

Emotional attachment.

So what I have done here is to create an emotional anchor. I have the prospect visualise and become engaged with the proposed product. I have put myself in their shoes, I have isolated the problems with using pens and brought them forward to remind the prospect of some of the bad things that can happen with cheap pens.
All the way along I have also trial closed and use the yes ladder.
As a salesperson, your job is to identify problems and then provide a reasonable solution.

It's really that simple.

The rookie salesperson will start firing off about features and benefits without first identifying the problem.

There was a time I ended up with a gig selling phones, door to door for a new Telecom provider. This was in the 90s. It was a time when everyone had a landline home telephone. Some people had a portable cell phone. These were different times, now there is a bigger demographic for cell phones than there are for landlines.
Everyone hates someone knocking on their door especially someone that you could identify as a salesperson. You have just gotten home from work, parked your ass on the lounge, cracked open a beer in front of the TV.

I don't really remember the script that the sales company had given me because it just didn't work. They tell you, for security reasons that when you knock on the door you should announce that you are from a particular company blah, blah.
But they did give us an identification tag that looks like we had some kind of authority, when people opened the door they didn't really know who was on the other side, so I probably looked like I was from some company but not necessarily a salesperson.

So after knocking on the door, my spiel went like this...
"Hi my name is Guy I'm from (company) Telecom and I'm here because there have been some changes to the way the telephone system works now, these changes affect this location and you need to be aware of them."

Instead of having a door slammed in my face I now had someone eagerly listening to what I had to tell them.

"So what has happened is there is some new technology in your neighbourhood and it's fantastic news. Sorry I didn't get your name?"
"My name is Steve."
"Again my name is Guy, pleased to meet you, Steve."
"So the technology is to do with the way the phone's work, we now have the ability to have not just a cordless phone, but a cordless phone with an unlimited range. Steve, have you ever been talking to someone on the phone and needing to get out the door because you're going to be late for an appointment?"
"Yes."

I would then take out the small flip phone to show him.

"This is some brilliant technology it looks and works like the latest cell phone, but it also works as a home phone for the cost of a local call, everything you do with your current home phone this phone does. Not only that it has the ability to store phone numbers and contact details. The phone comes with two numbers a mobile phone number and a landline number. If someone rings the mobile number this phone rings, if someone rings the house phone number this phone number rings. Not only that, if you're on a house call you can jump in the car and drive for a few blocks before it will switch automatically to a mobile call, which is a lot different to a standard cordless home phone. That's pretty awesome isn't it Steve?

"So the network is already in place, but you need these special handsets to take advantage of it. Many people have contemplated getting a cell phone, but this phone is 2 in 1, I'm sure you can see the advantages of that can't you Steve?"

"Yeah, but how much?"

"Well we're doing a special deal, one for you and your wife as a package for just $35, there are cell phones on the market that cost way more than that with fewer features, so it works out to be a pretty good deal, doesn't it?"

"Let's step inside I'll run through the paperwork."

"What's this paperwork about?"

"Well your current provider does not have the technology so these phones are exclusive to a different Telecom provider, but you'll be happy to know that all local calls cost $0.10 Less than what you are currently paying."

So you can see that I have trial closed throughout the whole presentation, I did not come across as a salesperson, I came across as a solution provider. I kind of scared the occupant of the premises and got their attention. I became their top salesperson in 2 weeks!

Feel Felt Found

The 'Feel, Felt, Found' technique is a classic objection handling technique that most salespeople know about. How well you use it could make the difference between it working as intended, to effectively stun the objection in the customer's mind and move on from it, or alternatively coming across as patronising and increasing resistance still further.

Just be careful with it.

This classic technique goes like this:

Respond with "I understand how you feel." This is intended to empathise with the customer, that you have heard them.

Relate to them referring to someone else who felt the same way initially. You're letting the prospect know they are not alone, and that things can change.

Then relate to them how that person 'found' that when they committed to the contract or product, they got what wanted and they were left satisfied.

Here is an example..
"It's a very good vacuum cleaner but it's expensive, I don't really have $1,000."
"I really understand how you feel, I had this customer last week Steve who would suffer terribly from an allergy to dust. Initially he felt the same way, a thousand dollars is a lot of money."

"However, Steve was able to take the vacuum cleaner straight away and then Steve found with the easy payment plan that pays the vacuum cleaner off over 6 months, his life just got a whole lot better."

Super Early close

So you've been doing your presentation for a little while and the customer is asking a lot of buying questions…

"Can I get it in red?"
"How long does it take before it can be delivered?"

...and you have responded to these questions accurately, and they come across excited then it might be an idea not to go through every single detail in your presentation.

"Have you seen enough, to make a decision?"

Time machine close.

It's fun to make your item urgent. Sometimes you can come across a client that is very busy and has not had enough time to absorb all the information that you have presented for them.

Making your items scarce can help you to get the deal over the line. "The head office told me that we only have 5 of this particular model left and we have another deal about to go forward and I don't want you to miss out. Let's do the paperwork now and if you change your mind just give me a call and I will tear it up."

Or something like, "Do you remember the film The Matrix?"
Wait for a response. "Did you know that that film is now over 20 years old". Use this tactic when selling investments or insurance.

Productivity, competitive edge

If you sell coffee machines or a coffee machine service, software or things that boost staff morale and can give a company better productivity, or a competitive edge. It's good to observe children and animals even medical professionals to close deals.
If you've ever had to say no to a teenager who then goes away. They come back later and then explain all the reasons why they need a particular thing.

I think everyone has observed a puppy dog that sits on your feet when you're eating a meal with those adorable puppy dog eyes!

When you have an illness at the doctors when the doctor says " I strongly recommend that you take this particular medication."

Or " I think it would be in your best interests to have that operation."

It's a good idea to keep a journal of the best deal closes, and how to handle objections. If you can present your product or service and address concerns, it will minimise objections. You can anchor facts in your presentation.

For example, "We sell a lot of this model VAN, it was only last week when XYZ courier company put in an order for 150 of them."

Here, in one sentence, you have validated the quality of the vehicle, alluded to the fact that big companies deal with you so therefore you must be reliable.

Chapter 18 - Staying motivated.

It can be really difficult to sell every day, any professional sales manager should know this.

Monday is a good day to plan your week. Friday is a good day to review and make a report because they are not good days for selling.

If you constantly find yourself in a funk and miserable and depressed you might need to change careers or find a different product that you get excited about.

Play your favourite music in the car, or listen to podcasts. Get motivated about those things that interest you on your trip to those sales meetings.

Fear- False Expectations Appearing Real
When you're fresh selling a new product, sometimes the fear of rejection can get in the way, fear will ease over time as you become an expert in manipulating the prospect. You will learn the right things to say and when to say them through experience, in the beginning, it's just a numbers game you might get one in every 10 you might get 2 in every 10. Statistics will get better as you become more confident.

When someone raises an objection which is better off referred to as, a concern, make sure you thank them for bringing that up. It is the same way you would deal with a complaint. Repeat the concern back to the client.

"The damn photocopier you sent me keeps spitting out the odd blank page."
"Thanks for bringing this to my attention Stephen. So what you're saying is every now and then, the photocopier prints out a blank page. Occasionally this can be a problem if the wrong thickness of the paper is used or if the paper is not slippery enough, let me take a look at that for you now. It's my absolute pleasure to rectify this situation and I'm sure we can get it resolved really quickly for you."

Chapter 19 - Networking

Leave a good impression with your customers. Make time to go back and see your customer. Follow up on how things are going with the product. I would go back with a $50 prepaid Cinema card, or something like it, I will show them the card and say to them that I'm happy to part with it if they can give me 3 or 4 referrals and if I get a sale with those referrals I come back with the card.

Chapter 20 - Practice

If you're new to selling make sure you practice with a friend. Keep your goals in sight. The most common type of sales position is that with a reasonable retainer and great commissions. An example goal might be to have a trip overseas. Take time to break down how many deals it will take you to earn commissions for that trip. Make a plan that sticks to your goals.

I think commission-only sales jobs are for suckers, I believe that if the company does not have enough confidence in you, and they don't care about spending money to get that product in the market then they should just go to hell. In Western countries, slavery is outlawed and it really makes me angry that companies like to take advantage of other people. It's up to you what you do, if you have a sideline that brings in money and the commission is huge then it might be worth having a crack at it but don't do it if you rely on it to pay your bills.

Most of all, take time to have fun with it, most sales gigs can be very rewarding and time flexible. If you work for a small company they might not be able to handle too many orders all at once. Don't burn yourself out.

At the beginning, one of my sales gig was door-to-door cold sales. I found myself in the trap of spending whole days out in the field collecting hundreds of business cards and then finding that I did not have enough time to follow up the leads. The meetings could go for a couple of hours and perhaps an hour's driving between the next one, it was simply impossible to send out information via email to 50 prospects and then the next week try to have meetings with them all, let alone the company I work for being able to fulfill the orders. Don't overdo it.

Always remember to pace yourself and keep your mind clear and stress free.

Most importantly, do not take life too seriously, take breaks to clear you mind and try and enjoy your freshly tweaked sales position.

I sincerely hope you have enjoyed this book. I know you have learned a lot about selling in a short period of time, haven't you?

You would have to agree that it would make a great gift for your boss or a friendly colleague. I'm sure that special person would be delighted if you were to pop over to where you bought this book from and purchase another couple of copies especially seeing it is so reasonably priced. :)

About the author.

Guy Glas, has been involved in selling for 30 years. His first company, turned over its first million in its first 3 years. Guy is a Clinical Hypnotherapist, and has been an international DJ, with the ability to sell Nightclub Solutions, as well as his personal appearances. Guy has also created sales and marketing programs and is a digital marketing advisor for many businesses.

Manufactured by Amazon.ca
Acheson, AB